# WELCOME!

This ultimate guide is dedicated to celebrating all things BlackBerry. From the devices themselves to the applications, accessories, development platform and tips and tricks, we hope to bring you on a journey of discovery.

Whether you're a novice BlackBerry user or a seasoned pro, we hope this Ultimate Guide will appeal to you. BlackBerry has so much to offer business users and consumers alike, so we're hoping we can demonstrate the potential and open your eyes to new experiences and time saving or entertaining features.

Next time you're out and about – whether for work or play – take a glance around the room. Then take another look and focus more closely on the mobile phones the people around you are sporting. Chances are, many of them will be BlackBerrys. There's millions of them in circulation, with millions more being shipped every year, so the likelihood of spotting one in the wild is quite high.

Whether you need a BlackBerry to help you get the right balance between life/work, feed you emails, football scores or just generally keep in touch with friends, family and work colleagues, it's clear the BlackBerry is much loved. We'd even bet that it would appear on the list of items people would save if they had to abandon their house or take with them to a desert island.

Since the first two versions of the Ultimate Guide were produced, BlackBerry's parent RIM has continued to innovate, unveiling new devices – including a tablet computer – and new services for users to experience.

We've really enjoyed collating this information and hope that you get as much enjoyment out of your BlackBerry, not just now but in the future too.

Thanks for reading

**Clare Hopping and Maggie Holland**
Editors

# CONTENTS

APPLICATIONS 74

Dictionary.com esperar

Dictionary | Thesaurus | Recent | Word of

English Spanish

**esperar**, *verb*
to hope

1. When it means *to hope, esper*
is one of the classic cases of a
Spanish verb which requires the
subjunctive in the following clau

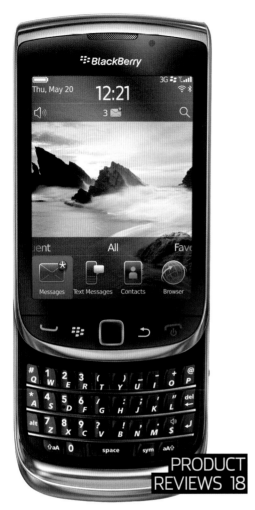

# THE ULTIMATE
# BLACKBERRY GUIDE

**EDITORS**
Maggie Holland
Clare Hopping

**CONTRIBUTORS**
Mary Branscombe, Simon Bisson,
Benny Har-Even, Chris Green, Richard Goodwin

## ART & DESIGN
**Art Editor** Steve Savage
**Photography** Danny Bird, Timo Hebditch,
Andrew Ridge

## ADVERTISING
**Advertising Manager** Jonathan Di-Sapia
020 7907 6281

**Marketing Manager** Claire Scrase

## MANAGEMENT
**Bookazine Manager** Dharmesh Mistry
020 7907 6100
dharmesh_mistry@dennis.co.uk
**Production Director** Robin Ryan
**Group Advertising Director** Julian Lloyd-Evans
**Newstrade Director** Martin Belson
**Chief Operating Officer** Brett Reynolds
**Group Finance Director** Ian Leggett
**Chief Executive** James Tye
**Chairman** Felix Dennis

**A Dennis Publication**

Dennis Publishing Ltd, 30 Cleveland St, London
W1T 4JD. Company registered in England.
Licensed by Felden 2009, and may not be
reproduced in whole or part without the consent
of the publishers.

Dennis Publishing operates an efficient
commercial reprints service. For more details
please call 020 7907 6281

Printed at Stones The Printers Ltd

ISBN 1-907232-41-9

**PRODUCT REVIEWS 18**

**ACCESSORIES 158**

recycle
When you have finished with
this magazine please recycle it.

# CHAPTER ONE

## INTRODUCTION

# WHAT IS A BLACKBERRY?

**C**ombining the features of a mobile phone and personal digital assistant (PDA) – the best of both worlds – the BlackBerry is miniature computer-like in behaviour, serving up as it does email, calendaring and other useful applications on demand.

The majority of BlackBerry handsets also have complete alphanumeric keyboards, whereas many PDAs and rival devices do not. Parent company Research in Motion has also served up touch screen devices for those who prefer life without QWERTY.

Every function of the BlackBerry – such as surfing the web, updating Facebook, sending a Twitter post or sending and receiving email – relies on, and works best with, an active data connection. The explosion in email use among business and consumer users can, in part, be credited to – or blamed on – the BlackBerry and its creator.

The BlackBerry evolved from a humble pager and was originally a business tool to help white-collar staff stay in touch with the office and keep on top of information such as share prices, sales, orders

and personnel matters.

Early models pioneered the use of mobile carriers for sending and receiving data long before the first BlackBerry included telephone capabilities. That is how important data is to these devices and to the people who use them.

Today, surfing the internet is a key function of all BlackBerry handsets, alongside text messaging and telephony.

But still at the centre of the BlackBerry is email and the innovative way the BlackBerry service gets messages to and from the handset.

Rather than the device periodically connecting to your server to see if you have mail, the server to which your BlackBerry device is paired will push new email to your handset when it arrives – saving battery power and minimising data use.

The email service works in two parts:

1. Via the BlackBerry device.
2. Email push, managed in one of two ways:
   - The BlackBerry Enterprise Server (BES), which works directly with Microsoft Exchange and Lotus Notes mail servers. BlackBerry Exchange Express (BESX) is a

free option of this software that can be added to a company's existing Exchange server. It brings all the functionality of BES, but is more affordable for smaller companies.

- The BlackBerry Internet Service (BIS), which is operated by service providers, such as mobile phone networks, to provide the push-email service to consumers with POP3 and IMAP mailboxes hosted by their home ISP or free providers, such as Microsoft and Google.

Whether you are a consumer or a business user, the BlackBerry experience is the same and key settings can be stored centrally, making it very easy for devices to be updated and reconfigured should they ever have to be replaced.

More recently, the BlackBerry has evolved into a very competent media player, capable of playing the most common downloadable video file formats, including DivX, as well as MP3 and Windows Media Audio files. The BlackBerry 9800 Torch is a great example of how RIM is expanding in the multimedia space.

# WHAT CAN A BLACKBERRY DO?

**F**irst and foremost, a BlackBerry is a mobile phone – and a pretty good one at that. But its capabilities do not begin and end with making and receiving voice calls, and sending the odd text message.

The BlackBerry combines the basics of a personal digital assistant (PDA) with a mobile phone – but then takes the concept further. Much further.

**Telephony:** Let's not forget that in addition to the myriad benefits on offer with a BlackBerry, it also functions very well as a phone. With superior call quality, built-in speakerphone to aid conference calling and Bluetooth support in many devices to aid hands-free accessory use, the BlackBerry is the ideal calling companion.

**Push email:** The cornerstone of any BlackBerry is its ability to send and receive email, with a user interface that can be controlled with one thumb. POP3, IMAP, Exchange and Notes email are all supported, with messages being pushed to the device as soon as they arrive in the user's inbox, rather than when the handset chooses, periodically, to look for new mail.

**Instant messaging:** If you use instant messaging to keep in contact with friends or colleagues when using your desktop, you'll like the ability to replicate this experience on the move. Regardless of where you are or what you're doing, instant messaging on the BlackBerry unites you with your IM contacts. With a familiar interface, contact management and notifications, messaging on the move will be as easy for you to use as it has always been.

**Web browser:** As mobile internet expectations have changed, so have web-browsing capabilities. Early devices sported a WAP browser with mixed reviews and the most recent BlackBerry handhelds are able to surf full web pages, delivering a quality experience akin to a shrunken down desktop.

**Pocket diary:** Manage your diary, address book, To Do lists and more from your BlackBerry device. If you work in a firm with Microsoft Exchange or Lotus Notes, you will probably be able to synchronise with your work calendars and contacts too.

**Mobile office:** You can view and edit Microsoft Office documents – as well as other popular work file formats, including Adobe Acrobat files – and all of the major image file formats while on the move. This should help make the most of any downtime, whether at the airport or in between meetings, helping to maintain that all-important work/life balance.

**Media player:** Your BlackBerry is not a stuffy work gadget, even if it was given to you by your seemingly stuffy firm. Alongside the business flavoured features, there is a powerful media player that can handle all of the latest video formats and provide the iPod with tough competition on audio playback. It can even sync with iTunes, and with the new UI, you

can seamlessly scroll through your music collection and watch videos in full-screen glory.

**Camera:** The latest BlackBerry units have cameras ranging from 2 to 3.2-megapixels. Devices such as the touch screen Storm also have auto focus and most have LCD flashes for low-light photography.

**Navigation:** Many BlackBerry devices now support GPS features as standard, making it easy to find your way to the latest work meeting or social event. BlackBerry Maps, for example, enables you to view details and directions in the palm of your hand.

Whether you need to find businesses, restaurants or something entirely different, BlackBerry Maps can help through step-by-step instructions and visual routes.

**Social networking:** Being able to tell the world who's just been rude to you or which celeb you've just spotted has become somewhat of an obsession thanks to the likes of Facebook and Twitter. And now you can keep the world up to date even when you're far away from your computer thanks to mobile support for social networking on the BlackBerry.

BlackBerry 6 has added a tool, allowing you to view all your social networking feeds in one place and post status updates and messages quickly. It adds even more ease to a fully rounded, web-based platform.

# BLACKBERRY vs OTHER SMARTPHONES

**M**ost smartphones, such as Apple's iPhone, Android-based devices, the Symbian-based handsets by Nokia or any of Microsoft's handsets, either Windows Phone 7 or earlier versions, can operate as standalone devices. There is no reason why they should not be able to access your email, surf the web and allow social networking or instant messaging.

But with alternative smartphones, the configuration lives on the device and the phone is doing all of the work.

However, each BlackBerry handset is associated with a server-side service that handles the process of pushing email to the device, rather than relying on the device to pull email from the server.

Pushing data to the device ensures battery use is minimised, as is data connectivity. It also means new email arrives on your handset almost as soon as it reaches your mailbox, not just when the device decides to look for it.

The BlackBerry service will be hosted and provided by either your mobile operator or your employer if you're using the device for corporate reasons.

There are benefits to this approach. If you lose your BlackBerry, it can be disconnected from your corresponding BlackBerry service, preventing further access to your data. It also means, if you replace or upgrade a handset, your data and settings can be pushed back out to the new device, saving you hours of configuration time.

RIM has moved on a lot from just producing functional devices that are first and foremost for sending and receiving emails. With the introduction of BlackBerry OS 6.0 comes an exciting new world for everyone, whether you want multimedia, social networking, apps, games, attractive hardware or instant email.

# HISTORY OF THE BLACKBERRY

**T**he story of the BlackBerry began more than a quarter of a century ago, when engineering students Mike Lazaridis (now co-chief executive) and Douglas Fregin founded Research In Motion (also known as RIM) in Canada, in 1984.

The company's early work focused on solutions and devices for the Mobitex wireless, packet-switched, data communications network in North America. Mobitex allowed for two-way, low-bandwidth, data communication, making it ideal for pager networks and, in particular, two-way paging, which let users receive messages and acknowledge receipt of these or even send replies. Early applications included point-of-sale (PoS) technology for retailers wanting wireless communications between in-store systems.

In 1996, RIM's first personal communications device was launched. The Inter@ctive Pager was a two-way messaging device for general use and quickly became popular among business professionals in several sectors, including healthcare and financial services. The company continued to focus on two-way pagers and early wireless modems until 1998, when the RIM 950 Wireless Handheld was launched. This was the first handset to look and behave like the BlackBerry devices we have today, but it still relied on Mobitex. As such, its use was limited to North America.

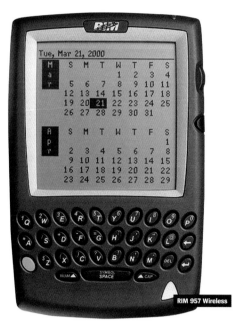

RIM 957 Wireless

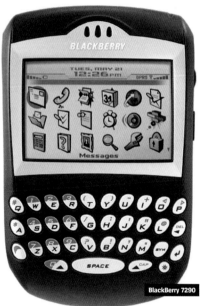

BlackBerry 7290

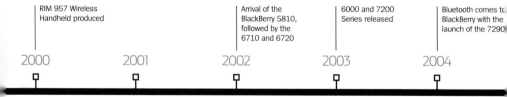

| RIM 957 Wireless Handheld produced | | Arrival of the BlackBerry 5810, followed by the 6710 and 6720 | 6000 and 7200 Series released | Bluetooth comes to BlackBerry with the launch of the 7290 |
|---|---|---|---|---|
| 2000 | 2001 | 2002 | 2003 | 2004 |

By 2000, RIM had come up with the RIM 957 Wireless Handheld. Its large, mono display and full QWERTY keypad set the format for more than a dozen future BlackBerry devices, although the name had yet to evolve. This came about after it was suggested the tiny buttons on the keypad looked like the seeds on a strawberry. However, a team of branding language experts claimed that strawberry suggested slowness, so the name morphed into BlackBerry. The device's original codename was PocketLink.

Success over the next two years, and growing international demand for its technology, led RIM to migrate its device range and software platform to the GSM/GPRS mobile networks, allowing its devices to be used almost worldwide.

In 2002, the BlackBerry 5810 arrived. The first device to carry the name, it combined two-way email and messaging with a basic mobile device. This was followed by the BlackBerry 6710 and 6720, which had more attractive designs and improved telephony features.

Following on from the popularity of RIM's business services, the company and its carrier partners created BlackBerry Internet Service (a version of the BlackBerry Enterprise Server) to enable mobile operators to provide a service that let consumers pull email from POP3 and IMAP mailboxes into a push email account. Then, in 2003, RIM released its next generation of handsets – smaller, cheaper, colourful and popular with consumers and business users.

The BlackBerry 6210, 6220 and 6230 were half-height, mono-screen devices that were low-cost and easy to use. These were followed by the 7230, 7210 and 7280, all of which had similar features to the

BlackBerry Curve 8320

BlackBerry Bold 9700

| 8700 Series appears, including the 3G 8707 | | BlackBerry Curve, with Wi-Fi and GPS, is launched | Bold, Storm and 8220 Flip hit the market | Curve 8900, Curve 8520, Bold 9700 and 9520 Storm2 launched | BlackBerry 6.0 announced. Torch 9800, Curve 9300 and Bold 9780 launched |
|---|---|---|---|---|---|
| 2005 | 2006 | 2007 | 2008 | 2009 | 2010 |

6000 series, but with colour screens.

In 2004, the 7290 arrived, bringing Bluetooth to the BlackBerry for the first time in a device the same size as the 7230.

By 2005, consumer demand for the BlackBerry was almost on a par with business use and more consumer-friendly devices appeared, including the 8700 and the short lived 8707. This was, technically, RIM's first 3G device, but it was not widely adopted by mobile players.

The BlackBerry Curve, for business users, and the Pearl, for consumers, were launched in 2007, with both handsets receiving updates that included GPS and Wi-Fi. A year later, HSDPA data was added as RIM brought the high-end Bold, Storm and Flip handsets to market.

2009 saw the release of the Curve 8900 (formerly codenamed the Javelin), BlackBerry Pearl 8120, BlackBerry Curve 8520 and successors to the first generation Bold and Storm devices in the form of the 9700 Bold and 9520 Storm2.

Following on from RIM's successes in the consumer market, the company has made a move this year into consumer-based devices that cover all bases.

The introduction of BlackBerry 6 in 2010 was a complete overhaul of the UI and was launched alongside the new BlackBerry Torch 9800 touchscreen device. Other notable devices launched in 2010 include the Bold 9780, Pearl 3G (9100 and 9105) and Curve 3G (9300).

The PlayBook tablet was also announced, sporting BlackBerry's QNX-based platform.

In the shift from an email device to a fully-fledged multimedia smartphone, the BlackBerry has blossomed into an all-round device and an impressive one at that.

It's not just the hardware that's changed though. The BlackBerry OS and UI has changed too, and with a new tablet platform in the mix with the BlackBerry PlayBook, we take a look at the development in the BlackBerry operating system over the last six months.

## BLACKBERRY OS 5.0

With the introduction of the new BlackBerry 9700 Bold and Storm2, we also saw the launch of a new OS for RIM, BlackBerry OS 5.0, that would filter out across a number of older devices including:

→ BlackBerry Pearl 8200 series
→ BlackBerry Curve 8330
→ BlackBerry Curve 8350i
→ BlackBerry Curve 8900
→ BlackBerry Bold 9000
→ BlackBerry Storm 9500
→ BlackBerry Tour 9630

The updated OS not only fixed bugs that appeared in OS 4.6, but also included a number of new services to make life easier, especially for business users under the command of an IT manager.

Tabbed Browsing made the BlackBerry's browser act more like a desktop experience. You are able to toggle through different tabs using the BlackBerry key (the one with the RIM dotted logo on it).

Date/Time were updated, allowing the time to automatically update to the country's time when you visited a new country.

Security Wipe was a new feature, allowing you to wipe all data from your BlackBerry including applications, emails, contacts and preferences if it was stolen. Although this was previously possible through BES, BlackBerry OS 5.0 added the function to BIS and BPS users too.

Mobile Backup first became available with OS 5.0. Like other mobile backup services such as MyPhone on Windows Mobile, all data can be backed up to a website automatically.

## BLACKBERRY OS 6.0

RIM has marketed BlackBerry OS 6.0 as a reinvention

of the BlackBerry platform, and although the Canadian manufacturer wants to ensure it's familiar to those avid BlackBerry fans, RIM also wants it to appeal to everyone, even those people who feel the OS hasn't changed enough in the last ten years.

BlackBerry OS 6.0 will come preinstalled in all the manufacturer's new devices, such as the Torch 9800, Style and 9780. It will also be available as an update on the following devices:

→ BlackBerry Bold 9700
→ Pearl 3G 9100
→ Pearl 3G 9105
→ Curve 3G 9300

The new homescreen UI allows you to change

and customise the homescreen according to the applications you use the most. You can add all your favourites to the homescreen so they're available with just a couple of taps or swipes.

BlackBerry Messenger adds more functionality so you can share all your experiences in real time, wherever you are.

An improved media player allows you to seamlessly scroll through your songs, view cover art and play videos in full screen mode, with pop up controls so you can get the most out of your media.

The Universal Search tool allows you to search your whole phone for a word or phrase, including files, folders and applications You can also search the internet, just by tapping one button.

Social feeds adds social networking to your BlackBerry. Like many other smartphone UIs, it presents a list of all your social networks in one place, so you can see exactly what everyone is doing at any time with one glance.

The browser has once again been revamped and it's faster than any other browser available. There's

tabbed browsing and the ability to use the browser as you would on a desktop, only smaller.

## BLACKBERRY TABLET OS

The BlackBerry Tablet OS is built upon the QNX platform, and as RIM's newest OS, it's built specifically with tablets in mind.

Although the QNZ microkernel can be seen in a number of different places, such as internet routers, infotainment systems, even to automate TV broadcasts, RIM's first product to use the OS will be the BlackBerry PlayBook, RIM's alternative to the Apple iPad.

Although not confirmed by RIM, it is thought that the QNX operating system could appear on future BlackBerrys. But when that will happen is a mystery.

Features of the QNX operating system include true multitasking, Adobe Flash 10.1 and HTML 5 support, with a much richer development environment.

Applications can be used across a number of different platforms, making it the most flexible BlackBerry platform yet.

# CHAPTER TWO

## DEVICES

# BLACKBERRY TORCH 9800

**R**IM's entry into the touchscreen smartphone market was a pretty disappointing one. The Storm had a screen that moved with every finger tap and the Storm 2's, although an improvement, was still a little uncomfortable to use.

RIM has decided to join the rest of the smartphone world with the BlackBerry Torch 9800 though, bringing forward its capacitive offering.

The 3.2-inch screen looks larger than its competitors because it's square rather than long and thin. At 360 x 480 pixels, it may not be the highest resolution, but this hardly means much - after all, it's what the display looks like rather than numbers, isn't it?

With 16 million colours, it's vibrant and bright. The best thing about that screen though is that it's hugely responsive, reacting to every slight touch.

The screen has also affected the typing interface, too. Of course you can opt to use the hardware keyboard (and what a fantastic keyboard that is), but the virtual interface has been tweaked too. Slide the hardware Qwerty in and the phone will switch to the virtual Qwerty mode.

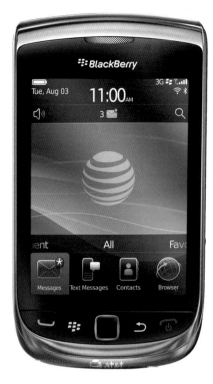

You can either type in portrait or landscape - switch between these by turning the device on its side. The accelerometer will instantly kick in and change the keyboard, making the keys larger and easier to use.

The text prediction tool offers up a list of words to choose from when you start typing. If you don't want to change the word, just tap space. To zoom in on a letter, press and hold the sentence. A slider will appear, allowing you to scroll through the text. One letter at a time is highlighted, making it very easy to make changes.

As everyday BlackBerry Bold 9700 users, we're massive fans of the BlackBerry OS, although it is a little glitchy on the BlackBerry Bold. BlackBerry OS 6.0 however, runs seamlessly. There's no lag when you're switching between applications or scrolling through the homescreens.

The homescreen has been completely re-mastered too. There are five screens you can scroll through by swiping through them and they're organised into favourites, all, media, downloads and frequent. We did find the screen to be a little too sensitive when scrolling through these, but it's not a massive issue and shows the sensitivity of the screen.

Tap once on the bottom toolbar to access the top row of apps, or once again to view everything on that homescreen.

There are also toolbars along the top of the homescreen. The top toolbar that shows your network, signal strength and battery remaining becomes the connections control screen where you can quickly turn all connections on or off by tapping on it.

The secondary toolbar shows your notifications and expanding this will show information about alerts such as text messages and missed calls.

These all feel a little Android-like, but it also means everything is easy to see and control from one place.

The browser is another new feature in BlackBerry OS 6. BlackBerry browsers have always been below the standards of other pre-installed browsers, and although the browser in OS 6 is a vast improvement, it's a shame not to see any Flash support. We can't slag off its speed though, although zooming in using multi touch sometimes resulted in a pause while rendering the page.

Tap and hold any link and up pops a menu. You can opt to open the link, open the link in a new tab (yes, there's tabbed browsing on the BlackBerry 6 browser), bookmark the link, send the link to a friend, copy the link to the clipboard, forward, refresh, switch application or go to the full menu.

It's an impressive set of tools and it's all set out beautifully. In fact, there's not much of the old clunky-looking OS remaining on the whole of the BlackBerry 9800 Torch.

Social Feeds is another high point on BlackBerry OS 6. Previously you could access Facebook and Twitter separately, but the Social Feeds brings them all together in one application. You can switch between your full social feed that displays any Facebook, Twitter, AIM, BlackBerry Messenger, Google Talk, MySpace, Windows Live Messenger or Yahoo! Messenger messages in one stream. Scroll to the left and you can view RSS feeds using a filter.

If you tap the toolbar on the Social Feeds app, you can switch between social networking accounts too.

In terms of media, the BlackBerry Torch 9800 features a 5-megapixel camera, with autofocus and flash. This is one area we weren't impressed with. The photos are filled with noise and although there's a whole host of options for improving photos, it's just not we would expect after the super camera on the BlackBerry Bold 9700.

Camera aside, the multimedia features of the Torch 9800 stretch far and wide. There's a podcast tool allowing you to download podcasts using BlackBerry Media Sync. It's really easy to set up podcasts using iTunes and then you can transfer across to your BlackBerry device using BlackBerry Media Sync. These will all appear in the Podcasts application on the Torch 9800 and will dynamically update when the next edition becomes available.

The music player displays cover art with track details and an easy to use music player interface below the cover art.

There's also a 3.5mm jack for headphones on the side on the Torch, although this means the jack

## Specification

| Dimensions (WxDxH) | 62x14.6x111mm |
| --- | --- |
| Weight | 161g |
| Screen | 3.2" (480x360 pixels) |
| Operating system | Blackberry OS 6.0 |
| Camera | 5-megapixel |
| Input features | Full Qwerty keyboard, track pad |
| Connectivity | Quadband, HSDPA, Bluetooth, Wi-Fi |
| Memory | 4GB storage, plus microSD card for extra storage |
| Battery | 1300 mAh Li-Ion |
| Standby time | 14 days |
| Talk time | 5.5 hours |

will stick out of the side unless you have the phone turned on its side.

Battery life on the BlackBerry Torch is impressive for a touchscreen smartphone, as you'd expect from a RIM device. Quoted standby is 336 hours compared to the Storm 2's 280 hours, despite the battery having a lower capacity. Our review sample was very impressive when keeping charge. After a day's usage, the battery had only gone down a fraction, despite having our Social Feed updating permanently, music playing on our commute and push email activated.

The BlackBerry Torch may be a chunk of a device at 111x62x14.6mm, but it has shot to the top of our BlackBerry chart. It offers everything you want from a phone, appealing to both touchscreen and hardware Qwerty fans. The one downside? That camera really needs to be sorted.

# BLACKBERRY CURVE 3G (9300)

**R**IM's BlackBerry Curve family is a happy one. And what better way to make the family even happier than a new arrival in the form of the Curve 3G (9300)?

Affordability, powerful and approachable were the three keywords surrounding the phone's announcement and, like its siblings before it, the Curve 3G doesn't disappoint.

Whether you're looking for a BlackBerry to help you be more productive on the move, to juggle your work/ life balance or just to help you keep on top of your social life, this could well be the handset for you.

"The majority of people in the worldwide mobile phone market have yet to buy their first smartphone and the BlackBerry Curve 3G is designed to provide an extremely attractive and accessible choice that will help convince many of them to make the leap," said Mike Lazaridis, RIM's president and co-chief executive.

"The new BlackBerry Curve 3G is a perfect choice for happily busy people who are looking for a user-friendly 3G smartphone to help them make the most of their day and to stay connected with their friends, family and co-workers."

Sporting a full Qwerty keyboard to keep text-happy users and those who need comfort as well as speed when it comes to typing smiling, the Curve 3G also packs in GPS and Wi-Fi, If you have larger-than-average digits, the size of the keys may take a bit of getting used to, but with a bit of practice you'll be replying to messages in the blink of an eye. It's not a major gripe and shouldn't prove a deal breaker for

this handset, but we thought it worth pointing out so users know where they stand from the start.

The optical trackpad also does what it's supposed to do, helping guide you in and out of apps and functions quickly and easily without issue. What's more, dedicated media keys will ensure you can access your favourite melodies while commuting to work, jogging or just trying to take some time out from the hustle and bustle of life. Our only gripe would be the slightly awkward positioning of the 3.5mm headphone jack.

Whether it's work files or songs you want to store, this device won't let you down as it supports up to 32GB in microSD storage. This is a godsend as the internal memory is a measly 256MB, which is more than a little pathetic.

The 2.4-inch screen is not as big as we'd have liked but it does the job effectively enough and powering through web pages is a nice, if not jaw-dropping, experience. We weren't very impressed with the camera either. Though at just two megapixels and sans flash, our expectations were set quite low anyway. It's handy as a backup for snapping in-the-moment pics of celebs you might see in the pub and so on, but don't expect to be blown away if you're a seasoned photographer.

Battery life is good. If you talk a lot or are always checking emails, you need something that doesn't drain overly quickly. Here it is. A whopping 19 days of standby are on offer with the Curve 3G, which is pretty darn impressive and we hope competitors are taking note.

The Curve 3G shipped with BlackBerry 5 OS but, of course, is now upgradable to the all-singing, all-dancing BlackBerry 6 OS and all the spoils on offer there, so we'd highly recommend jumping on the upgrade bandwagon to benefit.

## Specification

| | |
|---|---|
| Dimensions (WxDxH) | 60mmx13.9mmx109mm |
| Weight | 104g |
| Screen | 2.4"320x240 pixels |
| Operating system | BlackBerry 6 OS-ready |
| Camera | 2-megapixel |
| Input features | Trackpad, full Qwerty |
| Connectivity | Quad band (850/900/1800/1900 MHz ), Wi-Fi, GPS |
| Memory | 256MB Flash memory, microSD card support |
| Battery | 1150 mAHr removable/ rechargeable lithium-ion battery |
| Standby time | 19 days |
| Talk time | 4.5 hours |

# BLACKBERRY PEARL 9100/9105

The BlackBerry Pearl 3G (or 9100 and 9105 as it is also known depending on the keypad configuration) is a clear indication of BlackBerry's ever-growing mainstream appeal. With the arrival of this device, it's clear that RIM is focused on covering every type of mobile phone user there is.

Building on RIM's rich style heritage, the BlackBerry Pearl 3G is a looker. Compact and bijoux, it's hard to accept that this small handset packs in 3G and a host of features. Granted, those craving a full Qwerty keyboard will probably be a bit disappointed by this candybar handset, but that's not really the target market of this device.

"The BlackBerry Pearl 3G is unlike any other smartphone in the world and we expect a broad range of new and existing customers will be drawn to its powerful features and compact design," Mike

## Specification

| | |
|---|---|
| Dimensions (WxDxH) | 50mmx13.3mmx108mm |
| Weight | 93g |
| Screen | 2.25" 360x400 pixels |
| Operating system | Blackberry OS 5 |
| Camera | 3.2 MP camera |
| Input features | Trackpad, SureType |
| Connectivity | Quad band (850/900/1800/1900 MHz ), Wi-Fi, GPS |
| Memory | 256MB onboard, microSD support up to 32GB |
| Battery | 1150 mAh Li-Ion |
| Standby time | 18 days |
| Talk time | 5.5 hours |

Lazaridis, RIM's president and co-chief executive said when the handset was unveiled. "Considering the fast growing consumer interest in smartphones and the fact that more than three-quarters of the people in the global mobile phone market are still buying handsets with a traditional alphanumeric keypad, we think the new BlackBerry Pearl 3G addresses a substantial market opportunity."

He added "It allows consumers to upgrade their traditional mobile phone to a full-featured, easy-to-use and fashionable 3G BlackBerry smartphone that supports BlackBerry Messenger and many other apps while maintaining a handset design and layout that is familiar and comfortable."

Weighing in at just 93g, this is a highly pocketable device. And one you'd be happy to carry around with you and seen out with without fear or embarrassment in the fashion stakes.

The Pearl 3G exists as a platform between the two worlds of smart and dumb phones – a place, where those new to "smartphones" will be surrounded by familiar surroundings, such as the alphanumeric keyboard, but also have some serious power at their fingertips to boot.

The handset has a remarkably sharp screen and while it may only be 2.25-inch in size it is more than adequate for browsing the web, reading emails and using apps.

Let's be clear. The camera is not going to result in you throwing your compact away. It's 3.2 megapixels and does the job fine, but it won't serve as a full time replacement for the really snap happy.

But it's not all bad. Far from it. There's a host of connectivity options - HSDPA, 2G, 3G, Wi-Fi b/g/n and GPS - on offer that won't let you down when you need to make a call or check that important email. Indeed, the BlackBerry Pearl 3G performed admirably during our tests. We particularly enjoyed the browsing experience and, while the screen might be a little on the pokey side, it's sharp enough – at 360x400 pixels – for even the biggest mobile internet fans.

As with all new BlackBerry devices, the old-school trackball has been replaced with an optical trackpad – a law all manufacturers should abide by in our opinion.

We had no complaints about this input method, which is both agile and sensitive. In short, it's a welcome addition – kudos BlackBerry.

We were also impressed by the Pearl 3G's storage capabilities. It even comes bundled with a pretty beefy microSD card.

Couple this with the dedicated media controls along the top of the device and you have an aesthetically pleasing, media-oriented device.

Overall, the BlackBerry Pearl 3G is a very good phone. It has all the power you'd expect from a high-end device just without all the pretence – and this, for a lot of people, is a big deal. Not everybody wants a fancy touchscreen device, or even a high-end BlackBerry smartphone. Some users just want a device that doesn't pretend to be something else and allows them to check Facebook, send texts, make calls and receive emails when on the move without letting them down. The Pearl 3G is the answer here.

In essence, the BlackBerry Pearl 3G is the perfect device for those unfamiliar with the world of smartphones, looking to dip their toes in the water and see what they think. For smartphone virgins or users that want no-nonsense phones, this really is the perfect device, mixing both form and function into an affordable and rewarding package.

# BLACKBERRY BOLD 9780

**T**he BlackBerry 9700 was a massive success when it first arrived a year ago, because it really brought the BlackBerry into the hands of the consumer.

Now RIM has released the upgrade in the form of the 9780.

The BlackBerry 9780 is not a completely redesigned BlackBerry Bol. It looks pretty much the same as the 9700, and is equally as lightweight and exactly the same size.

The keyboard is brilliant, just like on the Bold 9700. Contoured keys make it easy for typing and prove that RIM is still the best at Qwerty candybars.

The screen is the same, although it doesn't look quite as vibrant as our 9700's – maybe this is because a 480x360 pixels screen isn't as exciting as it was a year ago, or maybe RIM just hasn't ramped up the vibrancy as much.

Screen aside, it's the internals that are more exciting.

The BlackBerry 9780 runs on Blackberry 6.0, and it's a huge improvement over BlackBerry OS 5.0.

For starters, the homescreen is more customisable and you can swipe between the screens using the hugely responsive touchpad.

Like on the BlackBerry Torch, the homscreens comprise All, Frequent, Media, Downloads and Favourites. Favourites can be customised so your most used contacts, apps and files are there with a couple of taps.

Universal search is a nice touch, allowing you to search any of your apps, files, contacts and folders, straight from the homescreen. To fire it up, just select on the magnifying glass at the top right on the screen and start typing.

The multimedia tweaks make it easier to scroll through your music collection, viewing your cover art along the way and the ability to watch videos in full size is great, although the 2.4-inch screen does limit some excitement.

Possibly the biggest change, aside from the OS, is the camera upgrade. We thought the camera on the Bold 9700 was pretty good for a company

## Specification

| | |
|---|---|
| Dimensions (WxDxH) | 60x14x109mm |
| Weight | 122g |
| Screen | 2.46" (480x360 pixels) |
| Operating system | Blackberry OS 6.0 |
| Camera | 5-megapixel |
| Input features | Full Qwerty keyboard, touchpad navigation |
| Connectivity | Quadband, Bluetooth, Wi-Fi , EDGE |
| Memory | 256MB onboard, microSD support up to 32GB |
| Battery | 1150 mAh Li-Ion |
| Standby time | 17 days |
| Talk time | 6 hours |

unaccustomed to multimedia, although camera technology has moved on substantially in a year.

Now the Bold's resolution has been upgraded to 5-megapixels, but numbers don't always mean a win, and the quality of the snaps were a little disappointing. They were noisier than we'd like, particularly in dark conditions and the flash tends to bleach most details out.

Although the BlackBerry Bold 9780 is an upgrade to the Bold 9700, we struggle to see why anyone realy feels the need to upgrade from a 9700. After all, when the latter device gets a BlackBerry OS 6.0 upgrade, it's only camera resolution in it, and who wants higher resolution noise?

# BLACKBERRY PLAYBOOK

**T**hose who own a BlackBerry, or are about to purchase one, will know only too well these devices are trusty ones, which blend style, sophistication and substance together in one package.

The BlackBerry in its smartphone form has been around for more than two decades, but it did come as a surprise to some that RIM has now diversified off the handset track to jump on the tablet bandwagon.

## A NEW BEGINNING

Of course, the BlackBerry PlayBook is no ordinary tablet. No siree. It's aimed mainly at business users – perhaps, given RIM's rich enterprise heritage, this isn't that much of a surprise – and sports and all-new tablet-focused operating system.

The web experience on a BlackBerry has always been a quality one but the PlayBook takes things one step further and one step higher. This is in part thanks to a lavish 7-inch (1024x600 pixels) WSVGA capacitive touchscreen with full multitouch and gesture support and partly due to the presence of a meaty 1GHz dual-core processor. Together with the new BlackBerry Tablet OS, symmetric multiprocessing is on the menu, giving users true multitasking ability so that they can be even more productive on the move.

In terms of web support, the PlayBook is a happy bedfellow with Adobe Flash Player 10.1, Adobe Mobile AIR and HTML-5. That means users will benefit from access to the sites and media they're used to on the desktop while out and about – with no compromise in sight.

## SECURE BY DESIGN

Security is also high on the agenda, as you'd expect from the makers of BlackBerry and from a device that has set its sights on the corporate world.

From the moment you take the PlayBook out of its packaging, its compatible with BES. You can pair your BlackBerry with your PlayBook so that content remains on your handset but can be viewed on the tablet. This means IT departments can happily roll out PlayBooks to employees in the field without worrying unnecessarily about security and the management concerns that come hand in hand with security.

## DEVELOPING A NEW WAY

Developers haven't been overlooked with this latest offering, either. Hand-in-hand with the PlayBook's arrival comes a stunning new development platform that offers new opportunities for developers to create new and compelling experiences for users.

Indeed, thanks to the QNX Neutrino-based microkernel architecture, the Tablet OS is highly scalable and features Common Criteria EAL 4+ security in addition to support for the industry standard tools developers are already more than familiar with.

C-based code can be easily ported thanks to full

## Specification

| | |
|---|---|
| Dimensions (WxDxH) | 130mmx10mmx193mm |
| Weight | 400g |
| Screen | 7" LCD, 1024 x 600, WSVGA, capacitive touch |
| Operating system | BlackBerry Tablet OS with support for symmetric multiprocessing |
| Camera | Dual HD cameras (3 MP front facing, 5 MP rear facing), supports 1080p HD video recording |
| Connectivity | Wi-Fi - 802.11 a/b/g/n, Bluetooth 2.1 + EDR |
| Memory | 1 GB RAM |
| Processor | 1 GHz dual-core processor |
| Standby time | TBC |
| Talk time | TBC |

POSIX compliance. There's also support for Java and Open GL for 2D and 3D graphics intensive applications and those written using BlackBerry's WebWorks platform.

## IN DEMAND
"RIM set out to engineer the best professional-grade tablet in the industry with cutting-edge hardware features and one of the world's most robust and flexible operating systems," said Mike Lazaridis, RIM's president and co-chief executive in a statement marking the tablet's birth.

"The BlackBerry PlayBook solidly hits the mark with industry leading power, true multitasking, uncompromised web browsing and high performance multimedia."

When you're not focusing on work, the PlayBook is an advocate of having fun and relaxing. It boasts high-quality multimedia features, including dual HD cameras to help you keep in touch with the world of work, play, or family and friends while away from home. In terms of audio and video playbook, the excellent player supports 1080p HD video, H.264, MPEG, DivX and WMV (video) and MP3, AAC and WMA audio files.

RIM reckons the PlayBook will be equally at home whether you're a one-person business operation or a massive organisation and we have to agree. At a centimetre thick and around 400g it's incredibly portable and just one glimpse at the device makes you want to touch it and carry it around everywhere with you.

# OTHER BLACKBERRYS

**W**e've reviewed the top new products from BlackBerry, but there are also loads more you can get your hands on. Some are US-only, and others are available in the UK, but there's limited availability.

## BLACKBERRY 9670 STYLE

The BlackBerry Style is the second clamshell device from BlackBerry. Following on from the BlackBerry Pearl Flip, it's only available in the US at the moment, and is aimed at fashionistas.

The BlackBerry Style has a slightly lesser spec than top of the range BlackBerrys, although you will find dual screens – the main internal display is 360 x 400 pixels, while the outside screen is QVGA resolution.

Running on BlackBerry OS 6.0, the Style doesn't miss out on any of the new features devices such as the Bold 9780 has, and with the same 5-megapixel camera, it's a multimedia hero too.

## BLACKBERRY TOUR 9630

The Tour collection of BlackBerrys has always been reserved for the US market and the Tour 9630 is no different.

The Tour 9630 features a 3.2 megapixel camera with 2x digital zoom and autofocus for taking some crisp shots.

The device also features 3G for super-fast surfing and everything's onboard including the top media player, BlackBerry Maps and the full suite of Office applications.

Like with the Bold series of devices, the Tour's keyboard is top, allowing you to speed type you way through emails, social networking and text messages.

## BLACKBERRY STORM2

The BlackBerry Storm2 is the second Storm series of devices, and it's a touchscreen device.

The screen features RIM's 3.2-inch SurePress screen that clicks as you tap. It's probably not the best screen out there, but certainly gives you feedback as you type on the large virtual Qwerty keyboard.

The BlackBerry Storm 2 also features 2GB internal storage, a 3.2 megapixel camera with autofocus and flash, plus HSDPA for speedy browsing.

The BlackBerry Storm2 is a great touchscreen option if you don't fancy the extra bulk from the Torch's sliding Qwerty keyboard.

## BLACKBERRY 8520

The BlackBerry Curve 8520 is a budget BlackBerry, but it's not budget in features.

The casing may not feel as premium as that on the BlackBerry Bold 9800, nor is there 3G, but you'll find Wi-Fi and EDGE onboard if surfing the internet is your thing.

The camera is a little cut back too at 2-megapixels, but it comes with the extra apps onboard including Office and BlackBerry Maps.

The screen may not be the highest resolution on the block at 320 x 240 pixels and 2.46 inches, but that doesn't mean it's not crystal clear. There's even the hyper-sensitive optical touchpad onboard for seamless navigation.

It may cost less, but that doesn't mean it's not a fully-functioning BlackBerry device.

# CHAPTER THREE

3

# BlackBerry

**12:21**PM
Friday, October 3

Messages

SMS

Contacts

Calendar

Browser

Maps

Media

Voice Dialing

Camera

Video Ca...

Instant Me...

Applications

Games

Downloads

Setup

Lock

# SETTING UP YOUR BLACKBERRY

**f you're already a seasoned BlackBerry owner,** you're more than likely already familiar with the basics of how to get your device up and running. But, don't just turn the page as this section still might teach you a new trick or two. If this is your first BlackBerry smartphone, this one-stop-shop will have you getting the most out of your handset in no time at all.

## EASY SET-UP

The real beauty of owning a BlackBerry is the fact that this is a device that wears many hats. Combining both style and substance, BlackBerry smartphones will ensure that you make the most of your time, whether you're at work or at play.

Indeed time-saving is at the heart of the device itself and associated BlackBerry solutions. Once you've set up your email accounts, for example, you won't have to do so again. If you upgrade to another device or lose your handset, the hard work is already done.

That's thanks to a server-side service that pushes email to your device and retains your settings, meaning minimal effort to configure a new handset. Importantly, for this to happen, you need to ensure you've set up your BlackBerry properly to begin with. Set-up is even easier for BlackBerry 6 OS-powered

smartphones. A short intro video provides a guided tour of the device, meaning you can get straight down to setting up the handset and personalising things to your tastes.

## EMAIL CONFIGURATION

This chapter will focus on configuring email accounts and other settings, assuming that your BlackBerry and its services are supplied by a network provider rather than your employer. Non-email features will apply to both types of user, but email configuration for business devices is very different. In most cases, your organisation's IT department will configure your device to talk to your Microsoft Exchange or Lotus Notes mailbox, but if not, the BlackBerry website can offer some useful hints, tips and support.

Once you're set up you'll be able to send and receive emails from up to 10 supported accounts. When you first fire-up your BlackBerry, it will run an initial wizard that lets you set information, such as the time and date, and do the basic configuration for your first email address straight from the device.

Some devices come with a pre-installed **Email Setup** icon on the home screen. If yours is one of them, simply click on the icon and follow the instructions. If not, all you need to do is:

1 Select '**I Want To Create Or Add An Email Address**' from the two options (we will deal with the BlackBerry Enterprise Server in a later section). Click '**Next**'.

2 The screen will explain the BlackBerry is going to open a web page to continue the configuration. Click '**Next**'.

3 At this stage, you won't have a BlackBerry web account, so you can go ahead with configuring an email account on the device. Select the **Email Accounts** link.

4 Select '**Add An Email Account**' from the list of options. If you do not have an email account, you can choose '**Create A BlackBerry Email Address**' to get a free email account linked straight to your device.

5 Enter your email address and password. Click '**Next**'.

6 That's it – your email account is configured.

You can also set things up from your computer. Visit **www.blackberry.co.uk/emailsetup** for operator-specific details.

If you are a first-time user, you need to create a username and password to access your mobile provider's BlackBerry web service. Just follow the on-screen instructions and you're off.

## IMPORT CONTACTS

A phone is nothing if you can't get in touch with the people that matter to you. Whether you need to communicate with work contacts, friends or family, ensuring your address book is up to date is key.

While transferring contacts from one phone to another can prove cumbersome on some devices, that's not the case with a BlackBerry.

You can store basic address-book information for hundreds of people on your SIM. You can also hold multiple records for each contact, such as phone numbers, email addresses, postal addresses and important dates such as birthdays and anniversaries.

If you previously stored names and numbers on the SIM card, you can continue to access these details straight from the card. However, it is easier to import that data to the BlackBerry.

From the Setup folder, choose the initial setup wizard, then select 'Import SIM Card Contacts'. You will receive a prompt to make sure you want to do this – select 'Yes'.

When this is completed, you can edit and add information to contacts, or merge SIM card

contacts with those synched with your computer.
Transferring contacts from Microsoft Outlook onto your BlackBerry is also easy.

1 In Outlook's **File** menu, select **Import and Export** to activate the associated wizard.

2 Select **Export to a File** then hit **Next**.

3 Select **Comma Separated Values** > **Next**. Note: If you are asked to install the Import/Export engine, you might require the Microsoft Office CD.

4 Select the **Contacts** folder with your address book in the **Export to a File** window > **Next** > **Browse**.

5 Once in the **Browse** window, select the location you'd like to save the CSV file to.

6 In the **Browse** window, choose a location where you want to save the CSV file > name it with the .csv extension > click **OK** > click **Next** > **Finished**

7 Import the CSV file into the BIS. To do so click on the **Address Book** link > **Import** > **Browse**

8 When the **Choose File** window appears, head to the saved CSV file's location.

9 Click **Open** > **Add** > The Outlook address book contacts listing will then appear in your BIS address book.

## SET UP WI-FI

The beauty of web and email-enabled smartphones is that they allow you to catch up on messages or surf the internet wherever you are, provided you're in range of your network signal or a Wi-Fi hotspot that is.

If your new BlackBerry has Wi-Fi and you are in range of a hotspot you have access to, you can use this to supplement the 3G or GPRS data connection. Given that Wi-Fi-based internet access is usually faster than even 3G, it will preserve your handset's battery life if the signal is strong.

Setting up a Wi-Fi connection is very simple and is also aided by a wizard. If the access point or hotspot you are planning to connect to uses WEP or WPA security, make sure you have the password, also known as a key.

1 Make sure Wi-Fi is switched on by heading for the **Manage Connections** area of your device.

2 Click **Set Up** Wi-Fi in the **Set up** wizard menu. After reading about how Wi-Fi can benefit you, click **Next**

3 Opt for **Scan for Networks** as this will sniff out any available networks in the vicinity. You can also search for connectivity by opting to **Manually Add Network.**

4 Your device will list the hotspot search results. You simply pick the one you want to connect to. If it's unsecured, simply connect. If it's secured, you'll need to enter the relevant password key. In either case, don't forget to save the settings.

5 That's it – you are up and running. Your BlackBerry will now connect to that Wi-Fi hotspot whenever it is in range.

# LINKING YOUR EMAIL ACCOUNTS

**O**nce you have mastered using your BlackBerry – and have customised and configured it to your liking – you might want to think about tackling the email setup.

## KEEPING IN TOUCH WITH THE WORLD OF WORK

RIM provides software that interfaces with a corporate Microsoft Exchange server to push work email to BlackBerry devices. But, if you have bought your own BlackBerry, with a service hosted by your network, you can still keep in touch with your work email as one of your 10, chosen, push mailboxes.

As with any email configuration, we recommend you do this via the web rather than your handset – it is easier. This is what you need to do:

[1] If you don't know the web address you need, go to the BlackBerry email service website, find your network and call them for it. For illustration purposes, we will use our fictitious network provider, Acme Mobile: *http://blackberry.acmemobile.com*.

[2] Log in with the username and password you created via the email setup wizard on your BlackBerry device.

[3] Click on '**Set Up An Existing Email Account**' and enter the email address and password you would normally use to remotely access your work email.

[4] After a while, the BlackBerry server will give up trying to auto-configure your email setup and will offer you the option to manually submit all of the settings. Select this option and click '**Next**'.

[5] Select '**This Is My Work Email Account**' and then click '**Next**'.

[6] The following screen gives you three options – select the third, under the heading '**Outlook Web Access**'. The actual wording of the option will be 'I Can Access My Email Account Using A Web Browser'. Click 'Next'.

[7] You will be asked for a variety of information. Note: this solution for accessing your Exchange email will only work if your employer provides webmail access to your Exchange email (also known as Outlook Web Access). Enter the webmail address you normally use. The username is usually in the form of domain/ email username (the name you log in with). Contact your IT department to find out what domain prefix to use. Use the password you

## Additional Information Required

We were unable to configure donkey_kong@dennis.co.uk. Choose one of the following options and select Next.

○ Re-enter email address and password.

**Email address:**

**Password:**

◉ I will provide the settings to add this email account.

[ Cancel ]  [ Next ]

**Picture 1**

use for webmail and enter your email address where specified. Finally, the mailbox name is usually the same as the first part of your email address, but, again, check with your IT department. Once all of this has been filled in, click '**Next**'.

⁸ As long as you have entered everything correctly, your Exchange email on your BlackBerry handset should now be configured and working.

## CONFIGURING YOUR CONSUMER BLACKBERRY TO TALK TO POP3/IMAP

For the vast majority of accounts, this will be as straightforward as putting in your email address and password because the BlackBerry server will work out the rest and configure your handset for you.

But a small number of email accounts will need to configure email from scratch and we are going to show you how.

Steps 1-4 are the same as for the Exchange setup, but the process changes at step 5:

① On the following screen, select '**This Is My Personal Email Account**' and click '**Next**'.

② From the two options you now have, select '**I Will Provide The Settings To Add This Email Account**' and click '**Next**'.

③ The following screen will ask for some basic information – your email username, password, email address and the name of your email server (if you don't know this, your email or broadband provider can tell you). Click '**Next**' when you have done all of this.

④ As long as you have entered everything correctly, your email should be working and flowing through to your BlackBerry.

**Set Up An Existing Outlook Web Access Account**

In order to configure your email account, we need some additional information. Please comp fields below.

Outlook® Web Access URL: http://webmail.example.com  ⑦
(e.g. http://exchange.domainname.com/exchange)
This is the web page address you use to retrieve your company using an Internet browser.

User name:  example/testuser  ⑦
(e.g. jdoe or domain\jdoe)

Password:  ••••••  ⑦
(Outlook or network login password)

Email address:  testuser@example.com  ⑦
e.g. jdoe@domainname.com

Mailbox name:  testuser  ⑦
(e.g. jdoe)

[ Cancel ]  [ Back ]  [ Next ]

**Picture 2**

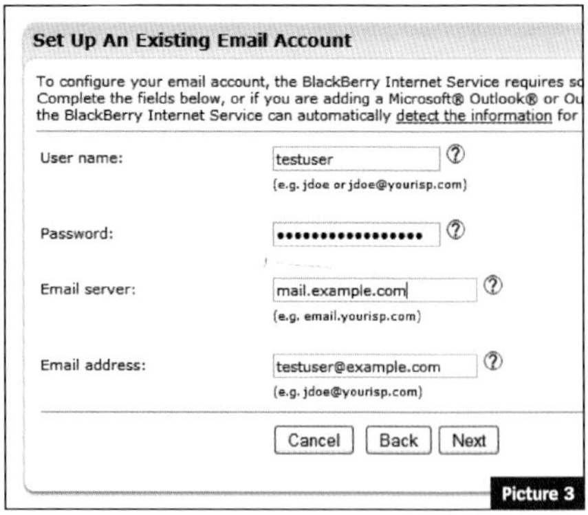

**Set Up An Existing Email Account**

To configure your email account, the BlackBerry Internet Service requires so Complete the fields below, or if you are adding a Microsoft® Outlook® or Ou the BlackBerry Internet Service can automatically detect the information for

User name:  testuser  ⑦
(e.g. jdoe or jdoe@yourisp.com)

Password:  •••••••••••••••••  ⑦

Email server:  mail.example.com  ⑦
(e.g. email.yourisp.com)

Email address:  testuser@example.com  ⑦
(e.g. jdoe@yourisp.com)

[ Cancel ]  [ Back ]  [ Next ]

**Picture 3**

# ADDING BLACKBERRY SUPPORT TO YOUR EXCHANGE SERVER

**There are a number of ways to deliver** services and information to your BlackBerry. The most common way for consumers is via a BlackBerry service hosted and maintained by their mobile phone carrier, using a product called BlackBerry Internet Service (BIS).

Using either your BlackBerry handset or a web interface, you can configure your BIS account to check your POP3, IMAP or Exchange accounts and to push copies of your mail to the device. This service can also keep your mailbox synchronised with the device, ensuring messages that have been deleted or read on your BlackBerry show up in the same way in your mailbox.

For business users, there is another option. Most companies have their own mail server, which is usually Microsoft Exchangeor Lotus Notes-based. Using BlackBerry Enterprise Server (BES), businesses can add BlackBerry push support to their existing enterprise email server, ensuring email, contacts and the company address book are accessible on their employees' handsets and always up to date.

Most people opt for Microsoft Exchange, so that will be our focus for this section. But every company's Exchange configuration is different, so we are not going to provide a generic guide to installing BlackBerry Enterprise Server. Instead, we will explain what you can do with BES to get the

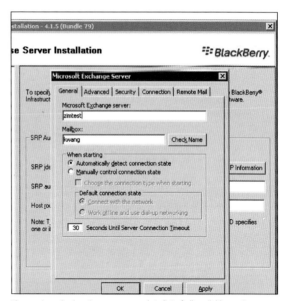

most out of the devices connected to it.

## AT A GLANCE MANAGEMENT

Business operations are no longer confined to office hours, office buildings or even the same geographic location. With sometimes hundreds or thousands of devices in operation, this presents a number of management challenges for businesses.

The powers that be need to be able to view the status of a network at a glance. An IT administrator needs to be able to see quickly whether the environment is healthy with a browser-style console that drills down to server level, group level and individual-user level, offering a consolidated view of all. The BlackBerry solution caters for these needs.

The services display gives you a complete list of all available service functions, explains what they do and shows whether they are in use.

## PUSH SUPPORT

All types of application – Java, browser-based or MDS Studio – can push data to a BlackBerry device. The IT administrator needs control to ensure the right apps are headed for the right users and that nothing untoward is going on. With BlackBerry, IT admins can specify which servers can push, as well as which users can or cannot have data pushed to them.

## SECURE APPLICATION CONNECTIONS

Security is a key concern for business users and consumers alike. Corporate security and authentication mechanisms – including proxy support, NT LAN Manager (NTLM), Kerberos and Lightweight Third-Party Authentication (LTPA) – can be extended to the BlackBerry. There is also support for RSA SecurID and HTTPS.

## ATTACHMENT HANDLING

An IT administrator can regulate which attachments are pushed to a BlackBerry device, minimising unnecessary data use and avoiding incompatible attachments being pushed. The Attachment

Server lets you set which filename extensions are permitted for pushing to a device and the maximum file size. Policies then allow the administrator to decide who receives attachments.

## GROUP-BASED POLICY ADMIN

If your organisation is big with lots of BlackBerry users it makes sense to put their settings into groups. For example, you could group sales people together, put field workers into the same grouping and ensure senior executives are linked. The BlackBerry supports more applications than just email these days and it might be necessary to push different information out to different groups. Individual policies can then be adjusted further.

## PHONE, SMS AND PIN-LOGGING POLICIES

For compliance reasons, organisations often need to be able to log calls and SMS use, as well as other types of communication, such as instant messaging and PIN-to-PIN messaging. With BES, you can centrally turn off the SMS function or use the console to log use so details of any exchange can be kept. In the world of banking, for example, this is a recommended practice. The BlackBerry is an asset of the company, but the company must be able to control its use, for which it can be held liable.

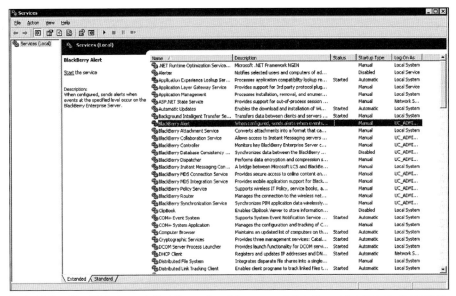

The installation of the BES Exchange plug-in guides you through the process, ticking off completed steps so you can see if anything has been missed or is incomplete.

## IT POLICY SUPPORT

BES comes with a sizeable list of default policies by which devices can be administered. Policies can be applied globally, by group or by individual user, allowing administrators to update and enforce the policies needed to govern a company's entire BlackBerry base.

## ROLE-BASED ADMINISTRATION

BES recognises there are differing levels of access required. A range of permission levels needs to be granted to take account of these differing levels of responsibility.

## REMOTE DIAGNOSTICS

The remote diagnostic capabilities of BES make it easy to see how devices are performing. The BlackBerry device can be locked or wiped remotely if it is lost or stolen, ensuring sensitive business information does not fall into the wrong hands.

## SIMPLIFIED ACTIVATION

A password can now be used for remote activation between BES and a BlackBerry device. Historically, if an organisation needed to get a new user up and running, that user had to be in the office so that their device could be set-up and configured. Now,

user can buy a device, phone the IT department for the password and get working right away.

Whether you need to set up and manage one BlackBerry device or thousands within a business, things are pretty straightforward. But if you need more intricate control over how the devices and users are supported in the field, the capability is there.

## BLACKBERRY ENTERPRISE SERVER EXPRESS

If you need similar corporate features to those provided by BES, BES Express could be for you. With no software licensing costs or additional overheads for individual user licences, this is a solution that provides advanced mail, calendaring and contact capabilities, enhanced security and remote file access. It also works with most BlackBerry and BlackBerry enterprise data plans.

What's more, you can quickly and easy get up and running with BlackBerry Enterprise Server Express. In fact, it's a very simple, four-step process:

1 Download the software
2 Choose your required deployment model
3 Install said software
4 Activate your device portfolio

# CHAPTER FOUR

 02
**12:21**
Thursday, May 21

EDGE

(3) Messages

# BLACKBERRY MAPS

**G**etting from A to B can be tough sometimes. Particularly if you've only just started working at A and B is a different place every day. But worry not. BlackBerry is on hand to help.

While stand alone equipment exists in the area of Global Positioning System (GPS), it's not always practical or financially viable to lug two devices around. While older BlackBerry handsets don't have built-in GPS - workarounds are available – most of the newer models feature this technology as standard.

Indeed, many users will find Blackberry Maps ready and waiting to be used on their device. And if their device has an older version, it's very easy to upgrade to the latest version by downloading an update from the BlackBerry website. There's a whole new world of places waiting to be explored. So what are you waiting for?

## WHAT IS BLACKBERRY MAPS?

BlackBerry Maps lets you pinpoint your location, find nearby businesses, restaurants and other places of interest, and then get step-by-step, visual directions to those places.

Rather than being stored on the handset, the maps are downloaded each time you fire up the application, so you should check with your mobile operator what costs, if any, may be involved. You will also need to be connected to the network to

use the service, but you're guaranteed to always get the very latest map data.

## USING BLACKBERRY MAPS

A good place to start is to find out where you are on the map. Once you have fired up BlackBerry Maps, press the menu button to bring up the context menu. Select 'Find Location' and the top entry should be 'Where I Am'. Press this to get a map of your current location. The device will bring up a 'Searching for Satellites' message, so it will work best if you are out in the open, with a good view of the sky, rather than in a built-up area.

If you want to find a particular address, choose one from your contacts book, from a list of recent contacts or from a list of favourites. This feature is particularly handy if you tend to search for the same things time and time again.

Another option in the menu is 'Local Search', which lets you enter a keyword, such as coffee, restaurant or hotel, and then searches for the locations of these services around the map's centre, up to a distance of around 30km. This is known as a location-based services search. Searching for 'petrol', for example, will bring up a list of petrol stations and the distance to them from the centre of the map. Select one of these stations and you will be given the address and phone number. Select the address and it will appear on screen. Highlight the phone number and

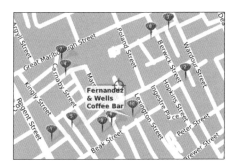

the device will offer to call it for you.

Hit 'Get Directions' and you'll be prompted to choose a start point and then enter a destination, which you can do using any of the methods above. You will then be asked if you want to plot the fastest route or the shortest route, and if you want to avoid motorways or tolls.

If you want to share your location simply select this menu option and the device will create an email, containing your coordinates, to which you can attach a message.

Users can switch between pan – which uses the trackpad to navigate around the map – and zoom mode – whereby rotating the trackball makes the image bigger or smaller – when using BlackBerry Maps. To orientate yourself, choose 'North Up', which puts North at the top. Alternatively, choose 'Track Up' to put the direction you are heading at the top. Once you have plotted a route, each stage of the journey will be presented in a numbered list – pressing a stage will bring up an image of it. Favourite locations can be bookmarked.

In summary, BlackBerry Maps has a number of strengths, including Local Search capabilities and Its handiness for walking directions. Whether you need to find a local restaurant for a business lunch meeting or locate that pub all your friends are raving about, this free application does the job.

# INSTANT MESSAGING

Instant Messaging (IM) is a great tool, enabling you to communicate with friends and family via messages that appear on their screen as you type and hit enter on yours. Its immediacy beats even email and, with their QWERTY keyboards, BlackBerry devices and IM are a match made in heaven. And it's a relationship that has stood the test of time thus far and looks set to last for a long time to come.

To complicate things, there isn't one messaging platform. In fact, there is a large number of competing ones. If you have a favourite desktop-based IM, the good news is your preferred network probably has a client for BlackBerry.

If your network-branded device includes links for these, you might expect to find your new application in the Downloads folder – after all, that is where applications such as Google Apps and Google Maps reside. However, on your BlackBerry, you'll actually find it in a folder called Instant Messaging, from where you can launch it and sign in.

RIM provides a helpful web page, http://mobile.blackberry.com. Scroll down until you find an icon called 'IM And Social Networking.' Click this and you'll be presented with a list of your favourite IM applications.

## BLACKBERRY INSTANT MESSAGING

Recent BlackBerry handsets have their own, built-in messaging application that works via RIM's servers, so you'll need a BlackBerry data plan for it to work. To use BlackBerry IM, you have to add contacts. To do that, you'll need your BlackBerry PIN, a unique number assigned to your handset that can be found by selecting 'Options' from the menu and scrolling down to 'Status'. Add it in, send someone a message and, once they have accepted you, the identifier will change from the PIN number into their name. You can also add and accept friends in a similar way using barcodes rather than PINs – a bit like shopping for new contacts!

It makes the experience feel like a special, members-only club that ensures only people who have your PIN can attempt to make 'friends' with you and vice versa. Once you have built up a contacts database, you will be able to send a message to multiple contacts at the same time.

If you're quite chatty and feel like your ability to say what you want is a bit restricted by the space limits posed by texts, the good news is that BlackBerry IM boasts an unlimited character length. That means you can type away as much as you like without being 'cut off'.

BlackBerry Messenger, or BBM as it's also known, includes other features too such as the ability to

personalise your user experience with a picture, real-time message delivery confirmation, the ability to group contacts for ease of communication and much more. The IM capability in BlackBerry 6 OS also makes it easier to have group conversations as well as providing information on when messages have been sent and/or received.

## GOOGLE TALK

Google Talk offers the same type of experience you are used to on your desktop in the palm of your hand. You obviously need a Gmail account to enjoy the benefits on offer, which include real-time chat, the ability to share pictures with your contacts, live status updates so you can share your mood and/or location, multi-chat so you can talk to more than one person at a time and personalisation options.

## AOL INSTANT MESSENGER

AOL Instant Messenger (AIM) is probably the most popular aspect of the AOL legacy. AIM on BlackBerry gives you full, real-time conversations, the ability to send pictures to other users, delightful emoticons and the facility to have several conversations at once. The program also keeps you logged in, so you are ready to chat at a moment's notice.

## ICQ

This is the original instant messaging service and was bought by AOL. But rather than scrap it completely, it's been kept alive alongside AIM, which is great news for ICQ fans. It offers real-time messaging, personalisation features and the ability to hold multiple conversations simultaneously.

## YAHOO MESSENGER

As with the other clients, Yahoo Messenger will pull your contacts list on to your BlackBerry, enable you to change your presence status and allow you to input custom messages. You can also invite multiple users into a single conversation and make use of avatars, emoticons and custom ringtones.

# DOCUMENTS TO GO

**Y**ou'll find three built-in Microsoft-Office focused applications tucked away in the Applications folder of most recent BlackBerry smartphones.

Word To Go, Sheet To Go and Slideshow To Go form part of the standard Documents To Go suite from DataViz, which lets you view and edit Microsoft Office files on your handset.

Be warned, while these apps are good and can help you be productive on the move, you shouldn't expect the full Office experience. After all, you are trying to view a document intended for desktop display on a device with a screen less than a quarter of the size of that of a desktop or laptop PC.

But there is still a lot you can do with Documents To Go. You can also upgrade to the premium version, which lets you do much more.

## WORD TO GO

→ The standard version will open, view, edit and create Word 97- 2007 for Windows and Word 98-2008 for Mac.

→ The premium version adds support for .docx files.

→ View and edit modes. Premium users can create new files too.

→ Read-only file support, with password protected file access in the premium version.

→ Integration with BlackBerry email application for opening attachments.

→ Text-editing features, including cut/copy/paste (rich text within a document), spellchecking and advanced character formatting (premium version only).

→ View/edit font types, sizes, colour and styling.

→ View tracked changes with premium users able to add comments.

→ Word count functionality, ability to add/delete tables and add/edit hyperlinks (premium version only).

→ Support for JPG, PNG, BMP, DIB, WMF and EMF graphics formats.

## SHEET TO GO

→ The standard version will open, view and edit Excel 97- 2007 for Windows and Excel 98-2008 for Mac. The premium version supports later versions.

→ View and edit modes. Premium users can create new files too as well as adding or deleting worksheets.

→ Integration with BlackBerry email application for opening attachments.

→ Support for Documents To Go IT policy group in BES 4.1.5, so IT administrators can manage document handling in a desktop-like fashion.

→ Read-only file support with password protected file access in the premium version.

→ Premium users can also sort, insert and edit comments and format cells and numbers

## SLIDESHOW TO GO

→ The standard version will open, view and edit PowerPoint 97- 2007 for Windows and PowerPoint 98-2008 for Mac. The premium version supports later versions.

→ View and edit modes. Premium users can create new files too.

→ Slide, Outline and Notes views.

→ Read-only file support with password protected file access in the premium version.

→ Integration with BlackBerry email application for opening attachments.

→ Premium users can view speaker notes and add, duplicate and delete slides.

→ JPG, PNG, BMP, DIB, WMF and EMF graphics support.

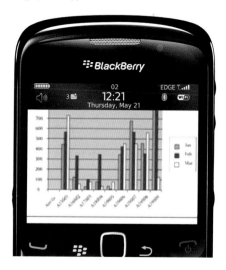

# SOCIAL NETWORKING

**S**ocial networking has and will transformed the way we live, work and play. Whether you're a fan or not, the ability to tell the world what we're doing, how we feel and what's on our minds is very empowering.

Users crave the same type of social networking experience they're used to on their desktop on mobile devices. Thankfully BlackBerry can help satisfy that hunger for 24/7 social network access.

BlackBerry 6 OS, for example, includes the ability to view all your social and RSS feeds in one place, at a glance. With more and more of us connected to more than one social network, this centralised status update feed means you won't miss out on what your friends are up to, whether they're into BBM, Facebook, Twitter or all of the above.

You only have to update your status once and you can effectively syndicate that data to BBM, Facebook, MySpace and Twitter all in one go, or you can select just one or two using the tick box options. It really is that easy.

In the same way you can view contact details for people in your address box, Social Feeds allows you to view all your interactions with a particular person, at a glance.

It's a similar arrangement for the RSS feeds you're signed up to. You can gather them together in one place to keep you as time and information rich as possible.

If you're not using BlackBerry 6 OS, you can still benefit from some great social networking apps. Read on to find out more.

## FACEBOOK
This app keeps you up to speed with friends' activities. You can also receive instant home screen notifications and integrate your Facebook lists with your BlackBerry address book.

Just download the client – you need 64MB of available memory and OS version 4.5 or above - from BlackBerry App World or www.blackberry.com/facebook, or follow the preinstalled link on your device.

## FLICKR
You can share memories and pictures of holidays well spent or time with friends via Flickr quickly and easily using your BlackBerry.

It's so easy to use like its bigger, desktop-sized brother, letting you geotag snaps, tag and resize images and share pics with those in your BlackBerry's address book.

You already need to have a Flickr account – or sign up to one - to take advantage, as well as a device with BlackBerry OS 4.2 and above.

## MYSPACE
If you're looking for an easy way to post pictures, send messages and keep your MySpace friends updated on what you're doing, why and when, this is the app for you. In addition to group messaging, blog and bulletin functionality, you can also check out friends' profiles, accept new friend requests and generally be a bit nosey!

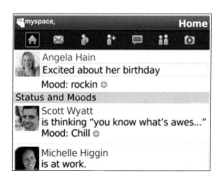

## TWITTER
This handy app lets you tell the world what you're thinking in 140 characters, just like the desktop version. The same tweet, RT and DM functionality is on offer, as well as the ability to upload pictures, post links from your BlackBerry's browser and much more. You need to ensure your device has version 4.5 or higher of the BlackBerry OS to use this app.

# GOOGLE APPLICATIONS

**G**oogle has become a familiar and popular face on the desktops of countless users worldwide. It's only right, therefore, for BlackBerry users to expect to see some of the tech giants applications on their devices. Thankfully, Google continues to develop and maintain software applications that make access to its key services easier for BlackBerry users.

## GMAIL MOBILE

The mobile version of Gmail provides users with a range of proprietary features that are not accessible via standard BlackBerry push-email accounts.

Although Gmail is most commonly used via the Gmail website, this application installs on to your BlackBerry handset – you can download it to your device by visiting http://m.google.com/ and clicking on the Google Mail link.

With Gmail Mobile, checking and composing messages is as easy as with the standard Gmail web interface. Many of the same features are available via the application, including the Gmail labelling and archiving feature, which you can't access in its true form via the email client on a BlackBerry handset.

You can make use of the handy search feature, flag-up important emails for ease of location at a later date, as well as reporting spam and accessing shortcuts and your address book. What's more, you can also manage multiple accounts from the one application, logging into all of them at once and switching between them quickly and easily.

## GOOGLE MAPS

Google Maps is a must-have companion to any BlackBerry device, even if you have BlackBerry Maps pre-installed on your device.

With this app – available from http://m.google.com - on your BlackBerry, you can work out where you are, find a given location and get a visual map of how to get you where you need to be.

You can get a satellite photography view and traffic information (where supported), and you can save favourite locations to speed up route planning. The application works anywhere for which the normal Google Maps website offers maps.

## GOOGLE MOBILE APP

This is a basic but very clever tool that creates a dedicated Google web-search box on your BlackBerry. The application can be moved to anywhere in your icons list, so you could have Google search just a click away on your BlackBerry home screen.

If you have installed the Gmail and Google Maps applications on to your BlackBerry, these will show up within the Google Mobile App, giving you one-click access to both, directly above the search box. To get the Google Mobile App, go to http://m.google.com on your BlackBerry and choose the Mobile App link.

## GOOGLE SYNC

Google Sync allows you to keep your BlackBerry calendar and address book synchronised with the information in Google Apps, providing Microsoft Exchange-like synchronisation for Google's suite. Simply put in your Google Apps username and password, and choose whether you want calendar, contact information or both pushed to your device. To get Google Sync, go to http://m.google.com using your BlackBerry and choose the Sync link.

My Location: London SW1W 9

# CHAPTER FIVE

 02
**12:21**
Thursday, May 21

EDGE

(3) Messages

# DESKTOP SYNCHING

**W**e live in a world where we spend **more** of our time out and about using mobile devices to keep in touch with friends and the world of work or to capture memories by updating our Facebook and Twitter statuses on the move or taking snaps.

As such, it's important that life isn't complicated once we return to desktop land. We don't want our BlackBerry and computer to be at odds. They should be synchronising key information, quickly and easily so that the user experience is somewhat seamless.While data such as email will happily download to your BlackBerry over the air – via Wi-Fi or the mobile network – a significant chunk of information requires conventional synching with your desktop or laptop machine.

You can synchronise tasks, memos, contacts and calendar entries so they appear in the same way on your handheld as in your desktop email client.

The required BlackBerry desktop software is either bundled with your handset or easily

downloaded from the BlackBerry website. The latest version is 6.0, which boasts an enhanced features set as well as an interface overhaul.

The software offers a reasonable degree of customisation and also ensures many key features – such as backup – can be performed with a minimal amount of clicks and decisions. This reduces the room for error and minimises the risk of losing valuable data.

## APPLICATIONS

The desktop software provides a really easy way to keep track of what applications are residing on your BlackBerry smartphone. With an easy-to-understand interface, you can see at a glance what your app lineup looks like, add and remove apps and keep abreast of updates.

To add, delete or update an app:
1. Once your BlackBerry is connected to your computer, click Applications.
2. To install an app (.alx) saved on your computer, select Import files.
3. To delete an app, opt for the x icon residing next to the app's name.

4. To update an app, click on the + icon next to the app's name.
5. Review your changes in the Application Summary view > Apply.

## BACKUP AND RESTORE

RIM recommends that you regularly backup the data on your BlackBerry smartphone just so your information is not lost in the rare case that something goes wrong. Using the BlackBerry Desktop software, you can restore or backup device data. Both are simple processes that require minimal effort on the user's part but provide maximum benefits.

To backup data:
1. Once your BlackBerry is connected to your computer, click Device > Back up.
2. Click Full to backup all your smartphone's data and Quick to backup everything except emails. If you want to have greater control over what is and isn't backed up, select the Custom option.
3. If your smartphone has built-in storage that

needs to be backed up, ensure that the check box Files saved on my built-in media storage is ticked.

4. You can then change the backup file's name, encrypt your data or save your settings using the File, Encrypt and Don't ask for these settings again options.

5. Hit Back up and you're done.

To restore data:

1. Once your BlackBerry is connected to your computer, click Device > Restore.
2. Select the relevant backup file containing the data you need restored.
3. Click All device data and settings to get everything back or Select device data and settings to restore specific items.
4. If your smartphone has built-in storage that needs to be restored, ensure that the check box Files saved on my built-in media storage is ticked.
5. Enter the password if the file is encrypted and locked.
6. Hit Restore. NB: On-device files will be deleted before the backup restore is actioned.

## SOFTWARE UPDATES

Software is a bit like a car engine, needing occasional fine-tuning to run at its best. When updates are available for the BlackBerry Desktop Software, you'll be alerted on the home screen. Then, it's just a case of hitting the Update my device button and following the simple instructions.

Be warned: It could take up to an hour for the update to be carried out and you can't disconnect your BlackBerry smartphone from your computer during this time.

## SWITCH DEVICE

BlackBerry handsets are lost, stolen and, very occasionally, they break. More commonly, though, users upgrade to a newer model to get the latest features, handset styles and a phone that doesn't show the scars of heavy use. The Switch Device feature is just what you need if you want your new BlackBerry to behave just like your old one. But without the battle scars.

To carry out the device switch operation:

1. Once your BlackBerry is connected to your computer, click Device > Switch Device.
2. Click the relevant device icon > tick the Device data box to migrate device data and/or the Third-party applications box to move over any compatible third-party apps > Next.
3. Ensure the new device is connected once prompted. Click on the device icon and your data is then transferred over.

## SYNCHRONISE

You can decide which information, such as contacts, calendar entries, memos and To Do lists, you want

transferred on and off your BlackBerry. You have complete control over what's synched, how, why, when and where.

To set up the synchronisation of Organiser data:

1. Once your BlackBerry is connected to your computer, click Organiser > Configure settings.
2. Select the check box beside and organiser app in the Intellisync setup window, click Setup.
3. Click the organiser app on your computer in the Available desktop applications list > Next > provide synchronisation directions >Next > Finish.
4. Repeat the above steps to synchronise another organiser app.
5. Once set up, to sync the data, simply select Organiser > Sync.

## MEDIA SYNC

BlackBerry Desktop Software 6.0 comes with an inbuilt Media Sync tool to ensure that your pictures and music are stored safe and sound and accessible whenever you want, wherever you want.

Moving media files to and from your BlackBerry smartphone couldn't be easier with this latest version of BlackBerry's popular desktop synching software. As well as giving you easy access to your favourite tunes and snaps, you can also share albums with your friends and loved ones too.

Using Media Sync to create a playlist for your next gym trip or that big house warming party, is a simple process where you're completely in control.

To synchronise your music:

1. Once your BlackBerry is connected to your computer, click Music.

2. You can synchronise playlist or song data by ticking the box next to the relevant item.
3. Select All music if you want to synchronise everything.
4. You can synchronise a random selection of music by ticking the box next to one or more playlists and selecting the Random Music option, then clicking Sync.

To synchronise pictures:

1. Once your BlackBerry is connected to your computer, click Pictures.
2. Select the Computer Pictures option, then tick the boxes beside the folders containing your images.
3. You can keep your pictures in their original size by selecting Optimize and unchecking the box.
4. Click Sync and you're done. To make sure you don't miss out on the Media Sync benefits, make sure you meet the minimum system requirements:

→ Your BlackBerry smartphone must be running version 4.2 or above of the BlackBerry OS.
→ Your device must have on-board memory or a media card slot.
→ You need to be able to connect your BlackBerry to your computer using a USB cable.
→ Your computing must be running Windows Vista, Windows XP SP2 or later or Windows 7.
→ If you want to take advantage of the music capabilities, you'll need iTunes 7.7.1 or above or version 10 or later of Windows Media Player.

# USING NON-WINDOWS PLATFORMS

It's a common misconception is that in order to sync and transfer data to and from your BlackBerry you have to be a PC user. This is not actually the case, although you may have to do a bit of work to find the right software and drivers so your computer and BlackBerry can talk to each other.

RIM offers a very good set of Windows drivers and application software with its BlackBerry devices, and you will find the most up-to-date versions on its website, along with an application for the Mac. Although BlackBerry for Mac synching software doesn't come in the box for most devices, it is available to download from the RIM website.

A number of third-party developers have also created Mac-compatible programs to use with your computer to enhance your BlackBerry experience further.

## POCKETMAC MACTHEMES

One of the more fun things you can do with a BlackBerry is to change its desktop theme by altering the wallpaper and customising the icons. This used to be the exclusive domain of Windows users. But that's not the case any more.

PocketMac MacThemes For BlackBerry lets you transfer a theme from your Mac on to your handset. It is available from *www.pocketmac.com* for $9.95 and most types of BlackBerry are supported. So whichever model you've got, you should be able to make the device match your Mac's desktop.

## POCKETMAC RINGTONESTUDIO

This is another application from the PocketMac team and one that most Windows users would love to see ported to the Microsoft platform.

RingtoneStudio, which costs $19.95 for the second version from *www.pocketmac.com*, lets Mac-owning BlackBerry users compose, edit and export custom ringtones, in a similar way to the iTunes feature that produces ringtones for the iPhone.

The application allows you to create ringtones from practically any multimedia file and you can assign them to your friends, family and colleagues so you know who is calling before you've even picked up your phone.

## SYNCHING WITH A LINUX PC

A BlackBerry can be synchronised with pretty much any distribution of Linux, but you will need to do a bit of command-line work to accomplish a successful first sync.

If you just want to move files between devices, life is a lot easier, as we explain later in this section when we talk about the Mass Storage Mode. For anything more complex, you need to tackle Linux sync software...

Open-source projects Barry and OpenSync aim to provide more functionality than just moving data to and from a flash drive.

The Barry project (found at *http://sourceforge. net/projects/barry/*) is "a GPL C++ library for interfacing with BlackBerry handhelds". It comes with a command-line tool for exploring the device

Drag any of the following here to

Creating ringtone...

iTunes file

and a graphical user interface (GUI) for making quick backups. Its goal is to create a fully functional synching mechanism on Linux. With Barry, you can explore, backup and restore, and sync databases. However, there is some assembly required, so take a deep breath.

OpenSync is platform and distribution independent, and provides the all-important inter-operability between the Linux OS and the mobile device, in this case, a BlackBerry. OpenSync can be found at *http://opensync.gforge.punktart.de/repo/ opensync-0.21/*.

When you install OpenSync, make sure you are using version 0.22 or later and follow the order because you will need it to successfully compile Barry for BlackBerry interoperability.

Once you have installed OpenSync, we will move on to installing Barry, which is more tricky, so read the instructions carefully.

Download the correct package for your system from Sourceforge (*www.sourceforge.net*) or the OpenSUSE Build Service (OBS) page (*http://download. opensuse.org/repositories/home:/ndprojects/*).

On Sourceforge, packages are available for multiple versions of Linux, the current supported versions of which include:

→ Ubuntu Gutsy Gibbon 7.10
→ Ubuntu Hardy Heron 8.04
→ Fedora Core 7
→ Fedora Core 8
→ Fedora Core 9
→ OpenSUSE 10.2
→ Debian Stable 4.0

On the OBS website, packages are located in subdirectories based on each individual Linux distribution. Be sure to select the correct platform – in particular, look out for whether you need the 32-bit or 64-bit version of the code.

Barry is divided into multiple binary packages. For example, if you want the GUI backup program, you will also need the Barry library. For non-development systems, you will need:

→ libbarry0
→ barry-util
→ barrybackup-gui
→ barry-opensync (libopensync-plugin-barry onDebian systems)

For development systems, you will also need libbarry-dev. The Sourceforge site has a separate section for debug packages, which are only needed if you run into a bug that causes one of the above pieces of software to crash.

Finally, before you compile Barry, be sure to specify 'enable-opensync-plug-in', otherwise the compiled application won't work.

The first time you connect your BlackBerry and Linux machine with a USB cable, you may see a warning on your handset about there being insufficient USB power to charge it. Don't worry; you can make an adjustment, using the btool command, that will ensure all is well. Enter 'btool -h' via the

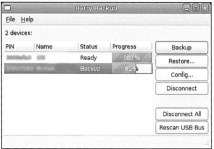

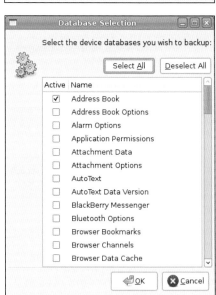

command line for a complete list of options.

The GUI backup application included with Barry is simple and effective. You get a small, but easy-to-use, display that shows the progress of the backup and which piece of information is being transferred.

The application will also show you the BlackBerry handset's device PIN (not to be confused with the security PIN number for the SIM card). The device PIN is used for bonding a BlackBerry to a BES or BIS server and for connecting BlackBerry devices together via the BlackBerry Messenger application.

Type in 'barrybackup' at the command line, wait a second until it finds your device and displays its PIN number, and, when it does, click 'Save'. You can edit the list of databases that the application will either backup or restore by selecting **Edit > Config** from the Option menu.

The software does require some basic knowledge of how to compile software for Linux, so it is unlikely to be to everyone's taste. However, the finished article works and will give you basic backup and restore capabilities.

## MASS STORAGE MODE

This applies to Windows and non-Windows machines, but shines when it comes to Macs and Linux devices.

When you connect a modern BlackBerry (one with an add-on flash-memory card) to a device with no compatible drivers, you will be prompted by the BlackBerry to decide whether you want to enter mass storage mode.

Mass storage mode makes your BlackBerry appear to the OS as nothing more than two USB hard drives. One is the built-in phone storage and the other is the flash drive, if you have one inserted on your BlackBerry.

No phone-specific features are accessible, but you can copy data to and from either of the storage drives, just as if they were a USB flash disk or hard-drive.

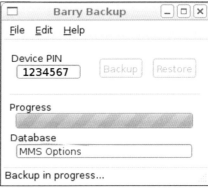

# SYNCHING ON MAC

**M**odern day computer users don't all fit neatly into one, simple category. Some use Windows machines while at work, Mac computers at home, vice versa or a complete mix of Windows machines, Macs or open source alternatives. As such, it's important that RIM caters to their differing needs when it comes to synching.

RIM offers Desktop Manager software for the PC and does exactly the same for Macs now too.

This means BlackBerry is much more attractive to all users, and is just as simple to use as the Desktop Manager on PC too.

Before you get started, it's important to note that BlackBerry Desktop Manager for Mac is only compatible with devices running on at least OS 4.2, ruling out much older devices.

You'll also have to ensure that you have OS X 10.5.5 or higher installed on your Mac, and have the relevant, supported version of iTunes (version 7.7.1 or higher at the time of writing).

Once you've ensured your equipment can be used with BlackBerry Desktop Manager, simply head to the BlackBerry site to download the software.

Once installed, you just need to plug your BlackBerry in to start feeling the benefits.

The first time you use BlackBerry Desktop Manager, you'll have to set up your device. In the Device Name field, enter the name you'd like to call your device. You can select the sync options you want to apply using the tick boxes next to the device's name and choose where you want to save music if you choose to sync your phone with iTunes.

## DELETING DATA FROM YOUR DEVICE

If you want to delete information for any reason, ensure you back up your whole phone to prevent losing vital data.

Connect your device to your computer and launch the BlackBerry Desktop Manager software.

On the device menu, select **Clear Data**.

You will now be given two options – **All Data** or **Selected Data**. For the latter option, select the items you'd like to delete.

To create a backup file for your device data, select the **Backup data before clearing check box**.

To encrypt the backup file, select the Encrypt backup file check box. Type a password if prompted/required. Click Clear and watch the data disappear before your very eyes.

## ORGANISER

You can choose to sync all data between your computer and BlackBerry device. Options that can be synched include contacts, calendar entries, contacts, tasks, and notes and memos.

Some devices can be synched over the air so you don't have to plug your device into your computer using a USB cable. For this, you won't need to use

BlackBerry Desktop Manager.

Before you use BlackBerry Desktop Manager for Mac, you'll have to turn on sync services on your Mac. To do this, head to the iSync application. Select **Preferences** in iSync. Select the Enable synching on this computer and you're ready to start using BlackBerry Desktop Manager.

To sync your organiser items with your computer and vice versa, select the information tab in the Desktop Software. Here, you can choose which options you'd like to sync using the separate fields such as Calendars, Contacts, Notes and Tasks. When you've decided which data you'd like to sync, click the sync button and the two-way sync will occur.

### BACKUP AND RESTORE

To backup data into the default folder on your Mac, just click the Back Up icon at the top of the screen, or the option in the main device settings menu at the top of your desktop screen. Click **All data** to save everything, and to back up specific data, click **Selected data**. Select the check box beside one or more databases. Click Back Up.

You can change the backup location of your data by entering the preferences tab on the BlackBerry Destop Manager application. Enter **Backup Location**, click change and type the new location.

To schedule automatic backups, click on the **Device Options**, then the **Backup tab**. Select Automatically backup when device is connected check box. Select an interval from the drop down box and decide what you want to backup, whether it's all device application data or add exceptions such as calendars or contacts which won't be backed up if you choose to tick that box.

To restore data to your device, you'll need mass storage mode turned on.

Please note, when you restore the data on your phone, everything will be wiped from your device before the backup file is restored. Anything you have not backed up will not be restored.

To restore your device after backup, simply click on the restore icon at the top of the screen.

Either select a backup file and then choose

whether you want to restore all data in the file or select some of it. For example, you may only want to restore contacts, so select that partition.

Click restore to start the process.

## APPLICATIONS

You can add, manage and delete all the applications installed on your BlackBerry using the Applications tab in BlackBerry Desktop Manager.

To add an application, choose the Applications tab at the top of the screen. In the list of available applications, you can select the checkbox beside the specified app to install it onto the device.

To choose a third party application that you've downloaded onto your computer, click the '+' icon and select the .alx file for the app. Click open and then start to begin installing the application onto your device.

To update applications, enter the Applications tab and click on Check for Updates. If there are updates to install, you can opt to backup and restore your data while the updates are installing or backup and restore the third party applications. Click start to begin the updating process.

To delete certain applications, enter the Applications tab and click the check box next to the ones you want to delete. Click start to delete the applications.

## MUSIC

You can sync your BlackBerry with your iTunes library using the BlackBerry Desktop Manager too. Playlists will be transferred, including podcasts and other audio files will be synched.

To sync your BlackBerry with your music collection, select the media section and then music. To sync all your music, select All Songs and Playlists. To sync only playlists, click Select Playlists and choose which ones you want. Finally, you can add a random selection of music to fill up any remaining space on your device. These songs will appear in the random playlist on your device once it has synched.

Click sync and your music will be on your BlackBerry.

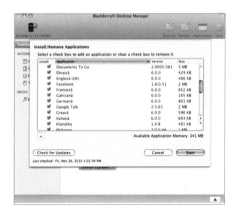

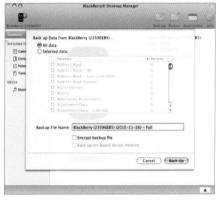

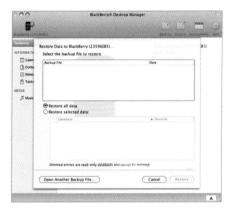

# KEEPING DATA IN SYNC

**M**ost of the time, your BlackBerry smartphone will operate perfectly happily on its own, pulling down data over the air as it goes along. Sometimes you will need to intervene to ensure your device and computer are singing from the same hymn sheet and we've already shown you just how simple that is for both Windows, Mac and other platforms.

If you're a business user, with Microsoft Exchange, Lotus Notes and BES in operation, things are even easier as everything is pushed to the device, not just email.

## MUSIC TO YOUR EARS

One of the more fun aspects of installing BlackBerry Desktop software on to your PC is that it provides a plug-in that lets you sync music and video from Apple's iTunes on to your BlackBerry.

| License Name: | |
|---|---|
| License Key: | |
| Register | |
| Server URL: | |
| User Name: | |
| Password: | |
| ☑ Contacts | |
| Folder Name: ./contacts | |
| ☑ Calendar | |

Many of the latest BlackBerry smartphones make excellent media players as well as mobile companions, so it makes sense to take advantage of them as portable MP3 or video players. And transferring music to and from your handset is as easy as pie thanks to Media Sync, which is outlined earlier in the chapter.

## WIRELESS SYNCHING

If you don't have access to a BES, there are third-party applications for over-the-air synching of data. The most common is SyncJe, which lets you synchronise your BlackBerry contacts, calendar and tasks with SyncML servers.

A plug-in installed on your desktop means data stored in, say, Outlook is kept in sync with a third-party SyncML server, which, in turn, communicates with your BlackBerry to enable wireless transfer of data that you would otherwise need to refresh over a USB-cable connection.

SyncML is a standard method to synchronise contact and calendar information between a handheld device (such as a mobile phone) and a computer. The specification includes support for push email, providing an industry-standard alternative to proprietary sync platforms such as the BlackBerry.

SyncJe costs between $40 and $70 (about £26 and £46) depending on which bundle you opt for and is available from http://mobile.nexthaus.com.

To benefit from the application, simply head for the above link using your BlackBerry's web browser. In the Over the Air downloads section, head for the one marked SyncJe for BlackBerry and click Download.

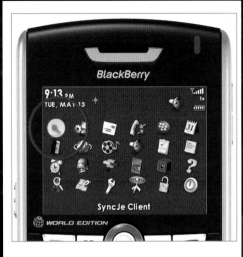

A message will appear telling you the download has been successful. If all is well, simply hit OK and head back to your applications menu where you'll find the latest addition in the form of SyncJe. Then it's just a case of getting the synchronisation details sorted in the Settings menu. If you prefer, you can also download SyncJe to your computer by visiting http://nexthaus.com/bb/BlackBerry.zip

## RECONCILE NOW

In the main menu within each of the email mailboxes on your BlackBerry is an option 'Reconcile Now' – and it is among the more useful email management tools on your handset.

Reconcile Now tells the BlackBerry to synchronise any changes (new/deleted email, calendar, memos) with the server. Not everything on the BlackBerry reconciles at the same time; for example, new email and calendar entries have a higher priority than address-book changes because these are more likely to alter on a regular basis.

Using Reconcile Now will force all changes to be synched, regardless of their schedule. Obviously, this can cause additional load on the server if run at peak times, so use it only when needed.

# CHAPTER SIX

## Applications & Developing
## for BlackBerry

**BlackBerry**

EDGE Y.dll

3 ✉* **12:21**PM
Thursday, May 22

**(3) Messages**

# BLACKBERRY
# APP WORLD

**A**pplications lie at the forefront of the BlackBerry OS -
without apps, the platform would be an empty shell
rather than a fully-funtioning smartphone.

There are a number of ways you can purchase applications
on a variety of third party websites, where there's a wider range
of payment options including credit or debit card.

There's a range of different applications you can download,
from business-based CRM applications, to social networking
clients, apps to improve photography and even fart
applications, just like on the iPhone.

BlackBerry's App World is RIM's offering to the apps

market, alongside the Apple App Store, Windows Marketplace and Android Market .

BlackBerry App World 2.0 was introduced in August 2010 and introduced a number of new features including BlackBerry ID, a single sign in and account system that can be used on both the BlackBerry client and the BlackBerry App World desktop storefront.

BlackBerry App World 2.0 also introduced credit card billing and carrier billing for AT&T Wireless subscribers in the US. This is in addition to PayPal that was previously the only option for purchasing applications,

BlackBerry App World is simple to use. When you launch the app, you'll see the feature apps along the top, and then underneath, categories, top apps, search and My World.

When you find an application you're interested in, simply click on it to find out information about that app, plus reviews, ratings screenshots. If you want to download it, click on the download icon.

The easiest way to pay for applications on BlackBerry World is PayPal, so if you don't already have an account, you're urged to set one up. As soon as you've paid securely for the app via PayPal or your credit card, it will start to download. You can watch its progress in the MyWorld tab. Once it's downloaded, it will automatically install.

If your BlackBerry doesn't come preloaded with BlackBerry App World, just point your browser to www.blackberry.com/appworld to download it.

App World currently has around 10,000 applications at the time of writing and it's increasing rapidly, although there's still a way to go until RIM's app solution will be a direct competitor to Apple's App Store or Android's Market.

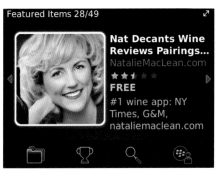

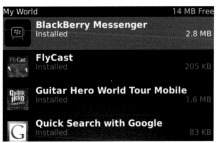

# DEVELOPING FOR BLACKBERRY OS 6.0

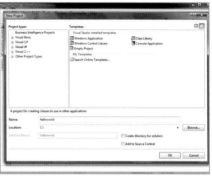

T he latest version of the BlackBerry OS, BlackBerry 6, has recently started appearing on devices. Initially rolled out with the BlackBerry Torch, it's a much-updated version of the familiar BlackBerry – with over 40 new APIs and many new user interface components.

It's probably BlackBerry 6's new UI that's most attractive to developers. There's a lot to be said for RIM's latest set of design features, which build on the existing BlackBerry UI, while updating it for touch and for a new generation of devices. That means not just tools for handling touch and gestures, but a new set of UI features and controls that work well with fingers. One big advance is the new context-sensitive pop-up menu, which brings common tasks into one touch-friendly place. It's a lot easier for users to work with a visual pop-up than for them to scroll down a long menu and select a single piece of text.

Another set of UI innovations in BlackBerry 6 mean you can work with more of the screen than before. Application title bars can now include device status information, including battery life and signal strength. You can also group common UI elements into toolbars, so your users will have one place to find key tools, simplifying working with BlackBerry applications and making them more suitable for use with the next generation of larger screen devices. Inside the rest of an application, there are now tools for working with tables and lists that simplify defining lists and working with external (and internal) databases.

One developer story that's gained a lot of publicity

recently is around what RIM is calling Super Apps, applications that take advantage of BlackBerry's ability to share information between applications – and even surface functions from one application inside another, adding items to menus. BlackBerry 6 adds more integration points, and more tools for bringing applications together. One big change is the introduction of a unified search model, which lets users search the web, third-party apps and their email, calendar and contacts from their BlackBerry's home screen. This means that applications can now advertise themselves as search providers, exposing their data to the BlackBerry search tools. Another feature that gets an upgrade is RIM's built-in BlackBerry Maps service. It's a lot easier to embed a map in an application with BlackBerry 6, with more tools for customisation – and even the ability to have several maps on the same screen at the same time. Other integration tools give you access to device sensors, so you can check to see if a slider keyboard is being opened, or if a device is being flipped over. Sensors are an increasingly important

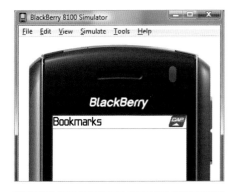

tool for mobile development, and RIM is helping developers access as much information as possible about devices (and their users) in this latest version of the BlackBerry OS.

Maps are only part of the BlackBerry 6 geo-location story. Location is an important piece of information that goes a long way to helping determine application and user context, and is being used by many new applications and services (with the popular Foursquare check-in service now a showcase BlackBerry application). You can use BlackBerry 6's built-in geolocation APIs to find a phone via GPS, cell-towers or WiFi, and a new set of APIs also mean that your applications can predict just when someone will get to a meeting – using a mix of crowd-sourced and historic information to predict traffic conditions. Mixing this information with device sensors gives developers even more context information, helping tailor BlackBerry 6 applications to their users' needs.

There's no need to learn a new development tool either, as the BlackBerry 6 SDK uses the same IDE as earlier versions, and can also be used inside Eclipse or Visual Studio, if you're making your BlackBerry applications part of a larger suite of tools and services. Java is still the main BlackBerry development language, and RIM continues to invest in tools and features, with the aim of simplifying and opening up application development.

One of the biggest changes in BlackBerry 6 is the arrival of a new WebKit-based browser. This means that you'll be able to use BlackBerry with HTML 5 web applications (including support for offline data), and also use RIM's new WebWorks CSS/JavaScript/HTML development tools to build local applications with web technologies. WebWorks opens up the BlackBerry OS to HTML applications, with JavaScript APIs for core BlackBerry applications – including the PIM tools. You don't have to write Java to deliver a Super App anymore; all you need are familiar web design tools and techniques. RIM's delivered JavaScript APIs that let web applications run in the background, so a website will be able to get out of the way, while continuing to update content on your device without filling up your screen.

# DEVELOPING FOR QNX (PLAYBOOK)

**R**IM's BlackBerry PlayBook is one of the most eagerly anticipated devices of 2011. With a dual core ARM processor and a wide screen 7-inch display, it's a light and pocketable tablet computer. However it's most definitely not a BlackBerry, running the QNX operating system instead of the more familiar BlackBerry OS. That means a whole new way of developing and delivering applications – in fact, according to RIM at the 2010 BlackBerry Developer Conference, the PlayBook will support several different ways for developers to write their code. It'll also support the App World - so there's a guaranteed delivery mechanism for your applications.

One option will be a Java runtime similar to that used by BlackBerry OS. If you've written a Java BlackBerry application for the latest phones it should run here. However the much larger screen size of the PlayBook will mean that your icons and graphics will be scaled, so you'll need to be careful about just how you design your graphic assets if you're planning on having your BlackBerry applications run on tablets as well as phones.

If you want to work with both phones and tablets, it's probably simpler to use WebWorks to write HTML/CSS/JavaScript applications. RIM has indicated that the two devices will share APIs, giving you the opportunity of using the same core JavaScript code on both form factors. You'll be able to use device detection techniques to deliver appropriate user interfaces for different size screens, taking advantage of the latest CSS features used by RIM's WebKit web rendering engine. While RIM is yet to announce details of the PlayBook's HTML 5 support, it's said that it will use the same WebKit browser as OS 6 phones which is already scoring well on common benchmarks (scoring 100 on the ACID 3 test). That means that well-design web applications will work with the PlayBook's large screen without needing a special mobile version.

Along with HTML 5, the PlayBook also supports Adobe's Flash. You'll be able to use Flash's video tools, without significantly impacting battery life thanks to Flash 10.1's support for hardware acceleration (and the PlayBook's GPU). There's a lot of Flash out there, and full support on a tablet means that sites that need DRM to deliver video (like the BBC's iPlayer) won't need to redesign sites and re-encode video to fall back to HTML 5. Flash developers will be able to use Flash's new multi-touch controls, and will be able to use Adobe's Flash Builder tools and the Flex framework to deliver more complex applications, including business tools that connect to complex back-end systems.

RIM is actively courting game developers for the PlayBook, and its QNX operating system supports native C++ development for the performance needed for the latest games. There's also support for the widely used OpenGL standard, simplifying porting games from platform to platform. Games

take advantage of the PlayBook's power, and there's additional cross-platform support for enterprise software, thanks to QNX's POSIX compliance. While POSIX doesn't mean that existing code will just compile on PlayBook, it does mean that it'll be easier to convert existing applications (especially UNIX and LINUX code) to run on RIM's tablet.

You can get started with PlayBook development right now, as RIM recently released a beta of what's likely to be its the primary development platform, Adobe's cross-platform AIR runtime. Demonstrated at Adobe MAX in October 2010, RIM's own user interface for the Playbook, along with many of its core applications are written using AIR. You'll be able to develop PlayBook AIR applications in Adobe's Flash Builder, or using your own choice of development tools. You'll be able to package cross-platform AIR applications to run on the PlayBook, minimising development investment, as an application written for an Android tablet will run happily on the similar-sized PlayBook.

Where the PlayBook's version of AIR differs from others is in its support for the PlayBook hardware and operating system (and for the bundled BlackBerry applications). RIM has worked with Adobe to add specific extensions to the AIR SDK, giving you access to the features you'll need to build complex applications that take advantage of the "super app" model RIM has popularised for the BlackBerry handset. These additional APIs include access to the

PlayBook's accelerometer, support for the PlayBook's touch gestures, and geolocation, as well as controls that offer the same look-and-feel as native applications. You can get started by downloading the beta SDK from RIM's website, and using it in conjunction with Adobe's latest Flex release and Flash Builder 4.

Once you've written and packaged your code, you'll need somewhere to test it. RIM's written a virtual machine-based simulator for the PlayBook, and you can use this to install and run your applications. The simulator has a development mode that lets you load applications over a network connection, without having to work with App World.

# DEVELOPMENT GUIDANCE AND SUBMITTING TO APP WORLD

**W**here most mobile device companies are content with giving developers just one way to build applications, RIM has three different ways for you to for write for BlackBerry. Business application developers can use the JavaScript-based MDS rapid application development system to quickly turn web services into form-based applications, while web designers can take their HTML/JavaScript and CSS skills and use WebWorks. However, most BlackBerry applications are built using the free BlackBerry SDK, a Java-based development environment with simulators for most common devices.

WebWorks is RIM's updating of the BlackBerry widgets platform, with support for the existing BlackBerry browser and the new BlackBerry 6 WebKit-based browser. While the company is working with open source phone tools like Sencha, JQuery and PhoneGap, to provide the best possible BlackBerry support, RIM has also open sourced the whole WebWorks platform. Once written, WebWorks apps can be packaged and distributed just like any other BlackBerry application.

BlackBerry's Java isn't the lowest common denominator mobile Java used by many device manufacturers. Instead, much like Android, it's closely related to the familiar desktop and server Java. The BlackBerry SDK includes a wide selection of commonly used user interface controls, along with APIs that give access to device-specific

hardware (including GPS and camera controls) and to the core RIM BlackBerry software. This last option is the key to what RIM calls "BlackBerry Super Apps", mobile applications that integrate with BlackBerry system software and with other BlackBerry applications. This approach lets your applications plug into the BlackBerry inbox and contacts, and use the BlackBerry Maps tools for navigation, something essential for CRM tools and for line-of-business applications. Other options let you use BlackBerry's push servers for business and consumer applications, delivering messages from servers and websites to Blackberry devices using standard notification features. Recently announced improvements to the BlackBerry SDK include the ability to integrate applications with RIM's BlackBerry Messenger peer-to-peer messaging service, an option that gives developers quick access to an existing BlackBerry-only social network.

RIM provides its own Java-based developer tools for Windows users, as well as support for the popular Eclipse development platform. We'd recommend using the Eclipse tools, as they're the future of RIM's Java development environment, and support more than just Windows – with a Macintosh version of the Eclipse plug-in announced at the 2010 BlackBerry Developer Conference. There are also a range of different device simulators that can be downloaded from the RIM developer website (http://us.blackberry.com/developers/

javaappdev/devtools.jsp), including support for the latest devices, like the BlackBerry Pearl 3G and the BlackBerry Torch.

Enterprise developers will also be able to use RIM's new BEAM tools, the BlackBerry Enterprise Application Middleware. This runs on both client devices and on servers, with a set of tools that simplify building enterprise applications, with BEAM handling data marshalling using an extensible XML framework that runs on any Java application server. BEAM's designed to simplify some of the more complex BlackBerry development tasks, including working with BlackBerry's push service.

While most developers will concentrate on building applications, the BlackBerry device UI is also highly customisable, with support for themes. You can create new icon sets and animated backdrops, using the BlackBerry Theme Studio. The latest version of Theme Studio includes support for timeline-based animations, and for slideshows, giving BlackBerry a Flash-like approach to theme development.

Java and web applications can be sold to end users through RIM's BlackBerry App World, along with themes. App World is easy to work with, and includes support for trial versions and for several different payment mechanisms – among them carrier billing,

letting users pay for their apps using their phone bills. RIM is extending its payment tools with the BlackBerry Payment Service, a set of tools that let you add micro-transactions to applications. This lets users purchase additional content, services and features without leaving their applications.

The BlackBerry Payment Service is just one among several different ways RIM gives you to make money from your applications. While selling through App World is the most obvious, RIM is also now offering its own advertising network. Adverts from the BlackBerry Advertising Service need just three lines of code in JavaScript or Java, and are delivered using RIM's own back-end. You'll be able to choose which of RIM's advertising network partners will be used, or you can just let RIM deliver a locally relevant advert from any of its sources. Revenues are split 60/40 between RIM and developers, and users will be able to click adverts to call, to map, to email, add to calendar, and to play video. If you're using advertising or selling through App World you'll probably also want to use the WebTrends-based BlackBerry Analytics service. This delivers reports that show you just how and where your applications are being used – and even just which features get the most attention.

# BUSINESS

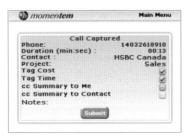

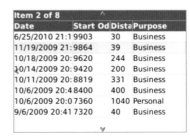

## CALL TIME TRACKER

Always on the phone to clients and then struggling when it comes to end of month billing to remember who you spoke to, when and for how long? Put that behind you with this free app that creates an Excel spreadsheet categorised by clients and projects. It remembers the details so you don't have to.

## HANDYLOGS MONEY - EXPENSE TIME AND MILEAGE TRACKER

A great way to keep track of spending, whether you're a busy executive, small business owner, or a consumer trying to stick to a budget. The premium version also offers additional features such as report generation, data exportation and archive creation.

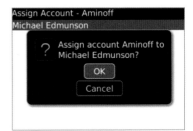

## DATABACKUP FREE BETA

If the information on your BlackBerry is important to you, this is the app for you. It quickly and easily backups up the personal data stored on your device onto your BlackBerry's microSD card. There's also a handy 'restore' option, which could prove a welcome friend in times of need.

## NICE OFFICE LITE

If you need to keep on top of emails and calendaring information wherever you are, you need a mobile office. Nice Office provides just that, letting you store documents online for use whenever you need, wherever you are. Data is synched wirelessly and easily retrievable should you lose or upgrade your BlackBerry.

## DUB CONTACT CARD

Paper business cards are so old hat. In this world of electronic communications, it makes sense for forward-thinking business people to have an e-card. DUB Contact Card zaps your contact data into your chosen recipient's mobile phone address book. It really is as easy as that.

## TUNGLE.ME

An easy way to arrange a meeting regardless of what systems other attendees might be using. You can propose a variety of start times, which are automatically adjusted to factor in different time zones if needs be. Organising a regular meet or one-off brainstorm never needs to be a headache again thanks to Tungle.me.

## WI-FI FILE TRANSFER

This app does exactly what it says on the tin. It's a secure and efficient way of transferring files between your desktop computer and BlackBerry, essentially transforming your handset into a wireless memory stick.

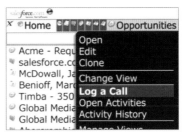

## SALESFORCE MOBILE

If you're already a Salesforce.com user, this app is for you. It offers you the familiar business tools you need in the palm of your hand so you can be as productive out of the office as you are at your desk.

# ENTERTAINMENT

| Iron Man 2 | | |
|---|---|---|
| **AMC Van Ness 14** 1000 Van Ness Avenue, San Francisco | | |
| **Tickets for 11:20 AM Sat, May 15** | | |
| ⊕ 2 ⊖ ADULT | 6.00 | **12.00** |
| ⊕ 1 ⊖ CHILD | 6.00 | **6.00** |
| ⊕ 0 ⊖ SENIOR | 6.00 | **0.00** |
| Convenience surcharge | | **3.00** |

## DAILY HOROSCOPE
If you like to be guided by the stars you can now do so at the click of a button thanks to this DailyHoroscope app. With Chinese horoscope listings, Druid horoscopes, zodiacal compatibility charts and more, this app is a must for those interested in what their star sign has in store for them.

## FLIXSTER
Film lovers everywhere will appreciate this app that will let them get their movie fix on the move. There's details of top box office movies, a plentiful DVD catalogue and film reviews from Rotten Tomatoes to boot. You can also search for film details by actor, director or title.

## PATTERNLOCK LITE
If you want to keep the data on your BlackBerry away from prying eyes, you'll need to lock it. But why not have a bit of fun at the same time? PatternLock offers you the ability to define your own lock pattern, which is visually appealing and looks more like a game than it does a security measure.

## BACKGROUNDS
This app puts more than 2,000 home screen designs at your fingertips. With multiple categories and new, unique wallpaper options added on a daily basis, this is the app you need if you want to feel like you have a different phone every day.

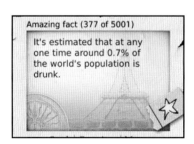

## FLASHLIGHT

It's dark outside and you need to get something from the garden. Jazz things up a little bit by using your BlackBerry as a torch. With eight colours and three brightness settings to choose from, FlashLight is fun as well as functional.

## 5001 AMAZING FACTS FREE

This app really doesn't need that much explaining. If you're happy to find out that 0.7% of the world's population is drunk right now, this fact finding app is for you. Both informative and funny facts are on offer, so there's something for everyone.

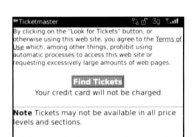

## TICKETMASTER

You've used the popular website to book tickets for your favourite pop star before but what if the tickets go on sale while you're in the back of a car on a long journey? That's where Ticketmaster for BlackBerry comes in. Same deal as the desktop version, just in mobile form.

## LEVEL

If you're into DIY, or just fancy messing around by seeing what surfaces in your house are actually level or not, this app has your name written all over it. Perfect for if you've lost your spirit level and the shops are shut.

# FINANCE

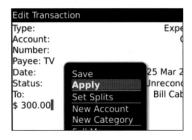

## MONEY FOR BLACKBERRY

Money for BlackBerry allows you to track your ougoings wherever you are.

After you've tracked all your day's transactions, you can export the data and sync it with your accounting software.

A number of different accounts are supported including assets, cash, cheques, bank, savings, investments, liabilities, line of credit, credit cards and loans.

## CALCULATE 4IN1

Calculate 4in1 is four calculators in one for your BlackBerry, including a mortgage calculator, car loan calculator, tip calculator and compound return calculator.

The mortgage calculator supports a number of different countries including the US, Canada and the UK.

It's all presented in an easy to use interface, so you can work out how much you'll pay in seconds.

## BLACKBERRY WALLET

BlackBerry Wallet helps make mobile online purchasing faster, easier and safer.

The application retrieves information from your BlackBerry such as your credit card number, shipping information, reward card numbers, retail website login details and gift card information.

It allows you to spend more time shopping and less time typing, making shopping online with your BlackBerry a seamless experience!

## MORTGAGE REFINANCING PRO

Mortgage Refinancing PRO will help you find out whether you should consider re-mortgaging your home.

You simply need to input how long you wish to stay in your home and how much it will cost you to refinance your home.

The calculator will then work out how much you will repay every month and whether the savings will be enough to recoup the cost of refinancing.

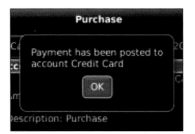

## BARCLAYS.MOBI

Barclays.mobi is a free shortcut application for Barclays customers.

Just click on the icon and you can access the Baclays mobile site straight from your BlackBerry's homescreen.

You can view your Barclays account details and balance, or view more about Barclays' products wherever you are.

Every page is optimised for use on a BlackBerry so you can view pages in all their glory too.

## MOBIACCOUNTS

MobiAccounts has been designed to maintain a good credit rating by managing your outgoings.

You can add transactions whenever you like, or duplicate transactions if you make regular payments for things such as a mortgage.

The application also calculates the next due date so you'll never miss an important payment and risk damaging your credit rating.

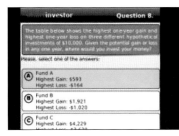

## SMART INVESTOR

Smart Investor is your own pocket financial advisor. The BlackBerry application will help you work out the best options for your investment, whether you're wary or a risk taker via a survey.

An extensive bank of guidelines then aim to advise you on a wide range of investments including shares, property, fixed interest, cash, private equity and art.

It's the perfect companion if you're new to investing or you just want to find out about alternative options.

## EXGIS EXPENSE AND MILEAGE TRACKER

Exgis Expense and Mileage Tracker allows you to keep track of your expenses and mileage on your BlackBerry.

It's one of the most downloaded finance applications on BlackBerry App World because it's easy to use and fully-featured, allowing you to customise client, project, currencies, locations, expense types, payment methods and mileage categories from one application.

# GAMES

LOTR: Middle-Earth Defense 1/5

## LOTR: MIDDLE EARTH DEFENSE

Protect Middle Earth from Sauron in this blockbuster game from Glu Games.

You'll have to position Aragon, Gandalf, Legolas and other characters from the game to defend strongholds from waves of enemy forces.

There are a number of genres to choose from, including story mode with 12 levels in five environments or Endless mode where you'll keep playing until you've run out of Battle Hit Points.

## TOUR DE FRANCE 2010

Following the Tour De France cycling tournament, you take the yellow jersey and be the leading rider as you race along the Champs-Elysees.

There are 21 stages of the fast-paced game and throughout each you'll need to manage your energy levels, visit the refuelling points, handle corners with perfection and pump up the energy while racing around mountain stages.

There are three difficulty stages – amateur, pro and legend and you'll need to win a number of jerseys to excel in each level.

## WATCHMEN: THE MOBILE GAME

Like Superheroes Alliance, the aim of the game in Watchmen: The Mobile Game is to become a vigilante and fight crime.

The game, based upon the comic and the film, sees you playing as Night Owl, battling enemies in New York City, or The Comedian in Vietnam.

Watchmen follows the original storyline from Rorschach's journal, making it a highly enjoyable experience.

## SUPERHEROES ALLIANCE

Superheroes Alliance is a free game that takes you into a world of superheroes.

Your job is to defeat villains, save lives, hire sidekicks and build an empire to become the greatest superhero of all time.

Superheroes Alliance is a community-based game where you join 150,000 other players to make the world a better place.

## WIN AT ROULETTE

If you head to the roulette tables when you hit the casino, Win at Roulette is the game for you!

The game for BlackBerry lets you play using either the US or European roulette wheel and gives you hints and tips along the way, training you to be the best.

Top graphics and sound effects top the game off, giving you a feel of being in a casino.

There's also a comprehensive guide for newbies, giving you the lowdown on rules.

## NEW YORK ROLLERCOASTER RUSH

Like rollercoasters? Why not sample up to 99 different tracks in Digital Chocolate's thrill seeking game?

Loop down Central Park, Downtown, Times Square and many other places in this game that takes an air tour around the city that never sleeps.

Attempt to get the best time around the tracks, and attempt to stay on the rollercoaster as your speed hits the maximum and you beat the best!

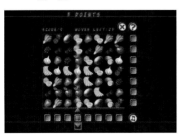

## DIG IN!

Dig In! is a collapse and collect game, where you have to collect and clear fruits and vegetables to make them into matching lines.

You can swap or shift lines to make them match and make them disappear

You're given a specific number of moves and if you don't complete the level in that number of moves, your game is over.

## GUNS 'N' GLORY

Guns 'n' Glory takes you back to the days of Westerns as you step into the shoes of Billy the Kid, Jesse James, and Butch Cassidy to recruit your own gang and brave Indians.

This game is all about strategy as you find the best position to ambush settlers, stagecoaches and the gold train.

If your enemy escapes, follow them until they're dead, or before they can tell the Sheriff what you're up to!

# HEALTH & WELLNESS

## FITNESS COMBO

Fitness Combo aims to increase your fitness and strength with a six week training program.

It will guide you to hit the goals by dedicating just 30 minutes per week.

The application will guide you through the steps needed to hit 200 situps, 20 chinups and 200 squats to make you super-fit and healthy.

## AN OFFICE YOGA

Want to get involved in yoga but don't have time to spend in the gym? Look no further than An Office Yoga.

The application will help you stay loose, supple and tension free while at work.

An Office Yoga mixes traditional yoga techniques with psychotherapy to get you relaxed as possible and boost concentration levels.

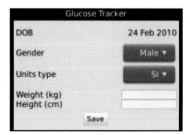

## DVT TRAVELCARE

Frequent fliers are more at risk from developing Deep Vein Thrombosis and this application aims to give a little advice on how to prevent it.

The app offers a personal risk assessment , advice and guidance to your level of risk, plus an activity program for you while flying.

## GLUCOSE TRACKER

Glucose Tracker does exactly what it says on the tin: it tracks your glucose levels and shows you all your glucose levels on a day-by-day basis.

You can enter notes to the calendar, such as sickness days or stress, either from a drop-down box or by entering text comments.

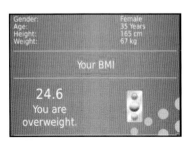

## BMI CALCULATOR

Although there are loads of BMI calculators available, Dr Hein Healthcare's is one of the most popular available on App World.

You can use the widget to calculate and estimate your BMI and work out your ideal weight if you have a high or a low BMI, taking into account your age and gender.

## BABY COG

Baby Cog allows you to track you child's daily activities to provide to pediatricians, or can be used by nursery workers to track up to 10 children to show parents.

Data can be exported by email and can be tracked for up to six weeks.

Data collected includes feedings, nappy changes, sleeping, activities and medications.

## QUIT SMOKING HYPNOSIS

If you're struggling to quit smoking, Quit Smoking Hypnosis is a top app that will guide you through the steps to stop smoking.

It's a single session that aims to help you become a non smoker and no longer have urges or cravings for cigarettes.

It will also break up the subconscious muscle habit pattern, stop food cravings as a result of quitting and give you a fulfilled feeling without cigarettes.

## TABER'S MEDICAL DICTIONARY

Taber's Cyclopedic Medical Dictionary defines 30 percent more terms than any other dictionary with more than 60,000 entries, 1,000 illustrations and 30,000 audio pronunciations.

When you download the BlackBerry app, you'll also have access to one year's use of the online dictionary at Tabers.com.

# IM & SOCIAL NETWORKING

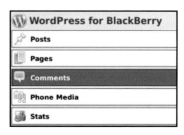

## BEREADER – GOOGLE READER

BeReader is a Google Reader application that allows you to read your feeds on your BlackBerry wherever you are and wherever you go.

The app always stays synched to your Google Reader account, so you'll never miss out on any news from your favourite websites.

You can add or remove feeds from your device and share links via Twitter, email and Facebook.

## WORDPRESS FOR BLACKBERRY

If you host a website on Wordpress, this is an essential application for your BlackBerry.

The application allows you to add and edit articles on your website using your BlackBerry. You can also upload photos and videos , plus manage comments, just as you can on the desktop version of Wordpress.

Wordpress for BlackBerry supports sites operating on version 2.9.2 or higher.

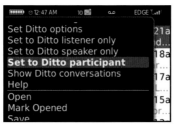

## DITTO

Ditto is a group text messaging application that works in the background of your BlackBerry from a server.

You tell the application which phone numbers are part of which conversation and then Ditto will route text messages sent by you and received from others to the entire group.

When you need to reply to a group, just reply to one person and everyone will get the same message.

## BLACKBERRY MESSENGER

BlackBerry Messenger is probably the most well-known messaging client for the BlackBerry. It comes preinstalled on most BlackBerry devices and the latest version allows you to send pictures and voice notes, a better user interface and a clearer contacts list.

The application allows you to IM groups of friends direct from your BlackBerry and works seamlessly.

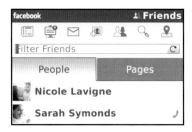

## TWITTER FOR BLACKBERRY

The official Twitter client for BlackBerry is the most impressive available on the platform.

It allows you to carry out all operations you can do on the browser-based application, including sending a message, tweeting people, reading streams, opening links and adding photos or videos to your tweets.

## FACEBOOK

The Facebook client for BlackBerry makes using your Facebook account from your BlackBerry a dream.

You can carry out all the operations you can use on the browser-based PC version and it's all presented in a stunning, easy to use interface.

Use the icons along to top to read your messages, view photos or search for a friends.

## SNAPTU

Snaptu is an all-in-one social networking application that includes access to all your social networks on one place.

You can use Twitter, Facebook, Flickr, Picasa, Accuweather, Sports, Movies, Sudoku and news from all major providers.

The best thing about Snaptu? It's free!

## UBERTWITTER

If you'd like to test out an alternative Twitter application, try out UberTwitter, one of the most well-known third party Twitter applications.

It supports a range of Twitter functions including photo integration, embedded videos, tweet shrinking, URL shortening, Twitter lists, saved searches, conversation threads, profile editing and retweet view.

# MAPS & NAVIGATION

## POYNT

Poynt can be used to find businesses, retailers, restaurants, movies and weather information in your local area.

The application uses either GPS or triangulation to get the most relevant results to you as quickly as possible.

You can find phone numbers, browse websites and get map directions with just a couple of clicks too!

## TRAVEL GENIUS PRO

Travel Genius Pro helps you find insider information on destinations, whether you're on holiday, have moved to a new area or just don't know about where you live.

The app will help you find out where you are and also add places to your favourites for future reference!

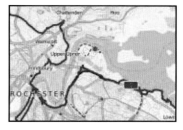

## TRAIN GURU

Train Guru allow you to plan train journeys, find out train times, ticket prices, view live departures and arrivals at stations.

You can make a particular journey or arrival your favourite too so you can quickly find the route next time.

Train Guru is presented in an easy to use way and it looks slick too!

## CYCLE MAPS

Cycle Maps highlights local and national cycling routes.

There's a cycle computer onboard that shows you your distance and speed and waypoint navigation so you can mark particular points on your route.

You can track your route and upload the map to the Cycle Maps website. You can even view your route on Google Earth if it tickles your fancy!

## LONDON CYCLE HIRE

If you use the London Cycle Hire scheme, this app is a must-have.

It'll provide you with information about where the cycle stations are, how many spaces there are in the stations, how many bikes are available to hire, where you are, plus you can view local and national cycle routes all in one handy app!

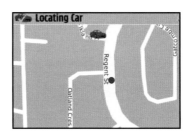

## VQ CARFINDER

VQ carfinder will help you find your car when you've parked in a carpark or use on street parking.

The app automatically remembers where you parked your car whenever you park.

When you want to find your vehicle, just tap a button and you'll be guided back to your car using BlackBerry Maps and GPS.

## WHEREABOUTS

You can track your whereabouts via GPS using this app.

You can track places you've visited with information such as latitude, longitude, horizontal accuracy, speed, course and date.

The application can use either GPS or triangulation worked out by how far you are from cell towers.

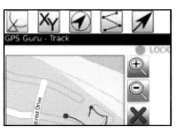

## GPS GURU PRO

GPS Guru presents you with maps wherever you are.

Features include your tracks shown on a map, cycle ways, walking routes, parks, bus stops and waypoints.

You can view maps whether you're on or offline and you can even view satellite views of areas.

# MUSIC & AUDIO

## SHAZAM

Shazam is one of the most popular music applications across all platforms. Shazam is a music recognition service that tags songs and allows you to download them and find out all the information you need to know about a song, artist or album.

You can also read reviews and watch YouTube videos direct from the application, or follow the lyrics if you want to sing along.

## PODTRAPPER

PodTrapper is a podcast tool that allows you to download and install all of your favourite audio and video podcasts in one place.

The app supports Wi-Fi and network downloads so you can download new podcasts wherever you are.

You can keep track of your last listened to podcasts and the sound will pause when you receive a call.

## WHITE NOISE

If you're having trouble sleeping, White Noise is the app for you.

The app plays ambient noise to help you get to sleep, whether you like listening to the sound of waves crashing on the beach, a running stream, crickets chirping or a rainfall.

The easy to use interface ensures you can pick a sound, change the volume and set off a shut offf timer in a few taps.

## NOBEX RADIO COMPANION

Nobex Radio Companion allows you to listen to all your favourite music stations on the move.

The app streams radio over Wi-Fi or through your network. Listen to songs with one click, or receive an email with a link to buy a song.

Social networking is supported, as is a shut off timer so you can choose to turn it off when you want to.

## 7DIGITAL MUSIC STORE

Browse the latest charts, preview the latest hits and discover, purchase and download songs with 7Digital Music Store.

7Digital also features a music player that imports all your music so you can listen to your own music collection with the easy to use media player interface.

## MP3 RINGTONE CREATOR

Want to make your own ringtones on your BlackBerry device?

Choose a song, find a starting point and save your ringtone exactly as you want it.

There are a number of effects you can add to your ringtones too, including fade in and fade out and you can adjust the volume too.

## ABSOLUTE RADIO

Listen to Absolute Radio's complete collection of radio's selection of radio stations including Absolute Radio, Absolute Rock and Absolute 80s in one place.

You can stream the radio stations through Wi-Fi or your network too, although the latter must be supported by your network.

## IO2GO

Io2go is radioio.com's radio station application.

The app comprises 75 radio streams across a range of genres such as Christian, classical and jazz, country, eclectic and speciality, electronic and dance, hip-hop and soul, holiday, Latin and tropical, pop and rock.

# PHOTO & VIDEO

## CAMERA PLUS

Camera Plus lets you capture, preview and email up to 25 photos in a photo album.

After you take your photos using the application, you can edit the photos to take the bad ones out, preview them in a photo album and send them using the email function.

## PHOTONOTE

Take photos, add notes and send them to friends with PhotoNote.

You can use the application as a visual todo list or as a photo diary and then share them through email or through your social networks.

## PICTURE PUZZLE

Set your creativity free with Picture Puzzle.

Take a picture and instantly convert it to become a picture puzzle.

All you have to do is move the individual tiles to rectreate the original picture in all its glory.

## SNAPSCREEN

SnapScreen is a screenshot tool for the BlackBerry.

The application allows you to take photos of your BlackBerry's screen and they're saved straight to your media card or phone's memory in the photos folder.

You can choose between saving your photos as jpg, png or bmp, according to your preference.

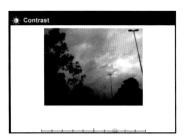

## PHOTO EDITOR

Photo Editor is another BlackBerry application for improving your photos.

Not only can you adjust the brightness, but you can also crop photos, rotate images or recolour it to get the best out of your BlackBerry's camera.

Once you've changed the picture, send it to your friends and family in a couple of clicks.

## SHOZU

ShoZu is a social networking hub that lets you upload your photos and video to more than 50 destinations including Flickr, Twitter, Facebook, Blogger and Photobucket for all to see.

You can also use the app to update your status, add details including tags and descriptions, and download feeds.

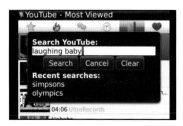

## PLAYER FOR YOUTUBE PRO

Player for YouTube Pro allows you to browse, play, search, share and bookmark YouTube videos on your BlackBerry.

You can also upload your own videos to YouTube using this app, as well as managing and viewing your videos and YouTube account.

## VLC REMOTE CONTROL

VLC Remote Control gives you the freedom to control your VLC player over Wi-Fi.

It allows you to select, play and navigate through videos using the familiar media controls.

You can view live updates of the VLC player progress bar, play status and playlist instantly from your device too.

# PRODUCTIVITY

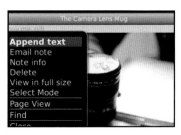

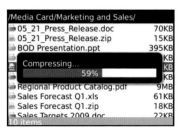

## REPLIGO READER

RepliGo Reader works with your BlackBerry email and your media card to bring your PDF files to life.

The application opens and displays PDF files natively. With page caching, your PDF files will load quicker and you can even copy and paste sections to send via email.

## FILE MANAGER PRO – ZIP AND FILE UTILITY

Most phones don't support Zip files, but this handy app will unzip all files and manage the folders too.

After you've unzipped files, you can edit them in native applications such as Docs to Go.

You can compress folders and files too, or manage other files using search, sort and other functions.

## EVERNOTE

Evernote is one of the most popular note apps available on BlackBerry and other platforms.

It allows you to jot down notes, thoughts, photos and recordings into one app and then syncs it all to your Mac or PC desktop.

You can search within the app for notes or media and even search for handwriting within photos, such as business cards.

## DETODAY

DeToday is an app that changes your Blackberry's homescreen into a Today Screen to ensure you have all the latest information where you need it.

You can import your appointments to the forefront of your mobile, change the colour and font size of items and even choose your own background.

## LOOKOUT MOBILE SECURITY
There are loads of security applications available for the BlackBerry, but Lookout Mobile Security is one of the best and it's free.

With antivirus, backup and find functions all included, you can be sure your BlackBery is safe wherever it is and whatever you're doing.

## BEEJOOSE
BeeJoose optimises your BlackBerry's memory to ensure you have enough memory for your device to run smoothly.

The app runs silently in the background and constantly monitors what you're using so it can ensure memory is always optimised.

## QUICK SEARCH WITH GOOGLE
Quick Search with Google gives you a shortcut to Google's search engine, allowing you to perform searches quickly in as few taps as possible.

Once you've typed in your search term the BlackBerry browser will pop up and display search results.

## FAST SCROLL
Fast |Scroll speeds up navigating around your BlackBerry using your volume buttons.

Simply press and hold a volume button and you'll rapidly scroll through lists.

You can also optimise your trackball, trackpad and touchscreen to work faster and with more precision too.

# REFERENCE & EBOOKS

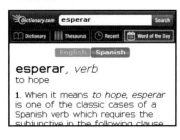

## DICTIONARY AND THESAURUS FREE

Dictionary and Thesaurus Free is a fully-featured dictionary and thesaurus in one.

The app features more than 500,000 words, definitions and synonyms.

There's also phonetic and audio pronunciations, spelling suggestions and Word of the Day.

## 100000 FREE EBOOKS WATTPAD

Wattpad gives you access to thousands of books, absolutely free.

There are more than 200,000 novels, fan fiction, short stories, poetry entries for you to download from the community-based site.

If you're a budding writer, you can upload your own writing too.

## OXFORD SPANISH ENGLISH DICTIONARY

The Oxford Spanish English Dictionary is one of the most comprehensive Spanish dictionaries available on BlackBerry.

More than 24 varieties of Spanish are covered and you can learn a little about the country's institutions, education systems and general life too.

## KOBO

Kobo is one of the most popular eBook sites available across platforms.

You can choose from more than two million affordable titles and thousands of free classics in the store.

Preview books if you're not sure you want to buy them and adjust text size to make them comfortable to read.

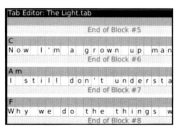

## CARNIVAL OF SOULS 1

Carnival Comics was the first comic book available on the BlackBerry.

The comic follows the tale of Azan Wild's Carnival of Souls, with each book split up into four sections for ease of reading.

The journey begins at a carnival, where the clown takes you hand as a guide...

## GUITAR STUDIO

If you're a budding guitarist, you'll need Guitar Studio to help you perfect your art.

You can download and edit tabs, view the chord library, take a look at song sheets and record, loop or playback your music from one app.

Learning to play guitar has never been so easy!

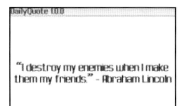

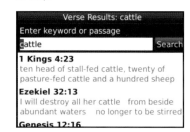

## DAILYQUOTE

If you're lacking inspiration in life, DailyQuote is one app you should download.

Every time you open the application, you'll be presented with a new quote, whether inspirational, insightful, or just a silly one liner, It's an app that will brighten your day, and it's free!

## BIBLE

Bible is the number one bible application on BlackBerry, and it's completely free to boot.

You can read the bible or share verses through Facebook if you wish.

If you're new to the bible, or want to read it again, you can set up a reading plan to help you get through it in an easy-to-digest way.

# SHOPPING

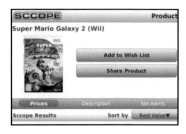

## EBAY

If you're already an eBay user, the BlackBerry app allows you to access the bidding site on your mobile phone.

You can find, bid and buy items, plus view you're my eBay account, monitor items you're selling and items you're watching.

You can also get reminders in your BlackBerry Calendar when a listing is about to end.

## SCCOPE

Sccope is a fully-featured shopping application that allows you to search for products by category, by barcode or by using text.

You can set price alerts so when the cost of a product drops, you'll get a notification.

There's a wish list feature to save all the items you want and you can share bargains with friends and family.

## HOUSE OF HOLLAND

Henry Holland is one of the UK's greatest designers and he's launched an app to support that.

The application features a bio of the designer, pictures from the catwalk and a shop where you can buy a number of different t-shirts within the app.

There's also links to press coverage, Twitter, Facebook and Henry's blog, plus a stockists page.

## SCANLIFE BARCODE READER

Scanlife Barcode Reader turns your camera into a barcode reader.

The reader can view Datamatrix, Ezcode, QR and UPC codes.

Once the barcode is scanned, the app will scour the web to find matching products, whether you're looking to buy or just want to find out more information about it.

## TESCO CLUBCARD

The Tesco Clubcard application for BlackBerry allows you to store your Clubcard on your BlackBerry in the form of a scannable barcode.

Simply scan in the barcode on your BlackBerry at the till and you can collect Clubcard points as normal.

You can also use the application to see how many points you have and the amount due in vouchers.

## FRUGALYTICS

Frugalytics is a shopping comparison engine for the BlackBerry.

If you're on a budget, you can make sure you pay the best price for anything you search for.

You can also read descriptions, and review ratings from all over the internet to get a fair view of the product you're looking for.

## OURGROCERIES SHOPPING LIST

OurGroceries keeps your shopping list up to date across different family members' mobile phones.

Whenever you add a new item, it will show up on your partner's shopping list so you can ensure whoever does the shopping knows what you need.

You can also keep track of key ingredients for your favourites recipes.

## CARDSTAR

CardStar stores all your card details, loyalty and reward card information in one place.

You can store numerous accounts and types including debit/credit cards, Sainsbury, Tesco, Blockbuster, libraries, associations and more.

# SPORTS & RECREATION

## SKY SPORTS LIVE FOOTBALL

Sky Sports Live Football helps you keep up to date with all the football scores wherever you are.

There's also live text commentary, live league tables, match stats, results, match photos, player profiles, team line ups and formations, a 'My Scores' area where you can enter your favourite teams and games to your calendar.

## SCOREMOBILE FOR BLACKBERRY

ScoreMobile for BlackBerry is a full sporting application. You can check on scores from around the sporting world, including baseball, football, American football, basketball and tennis.

You can add all your favourite teams to track exactly what you want to see too.

## SPORTS ILLUSTRATED

The Sports Illustrated application for BlackBerry brings the popular sporting title to your phone.

You can view stories, features and pictures all on your BlackBerry's screen along with the latest scores and rumours about what's going on in the world of sport.

## NAVITA SPORTS

Like ScoreMobile, Navita Sports tracks all the latest scores for most sports including football, tennis, Formula 1, basketball, hockey, football and rugby.

Game times will automatically adjust to the timezone and the app will remember the last page you were looking at.

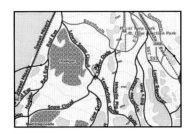

| FORMULA1.COM | | 📶 vodafone |
|---|---|---|
| | | STANDINGS |
| RIVERS | | |
| 'os | Driver | Pts |
| 1 | Lewis Hamilton | 127 |
| 2 | Jenson Button | 121 |
| 3 | Sebastian Vettel | 115 |

## FORMULA1.COM 2010

Track your favourite F1 teams, drivers and news on Formula1.com 2010.

The app streams real-time data from the Formula One Management Technical Facility at the racetrack.

You can also view all the data from each racetrack including air and track temperatures, humidity, air pressure, rainfall and wind speed.

## GPSSKIMAPS NORTH AMERICA

If you're a keen skier, GpsSkiMaps is the app for you.

It offers maps of five major US ski resorts and allows you to track analytics and stats for each of your runs.

You can pan, zoom and locate yourself on a run and record your GPS tracks for future reference.

## SPEEDOMETER

Track your speed whenever you're on a bus, train or just walking.

Speedometer allows you to switch between measurements, whether you want your speed tracked in kilometres per hour or miles per hour.

There's even the option to keep your phone's backlight on for continuous tracking.

## GOLF GENIE PRO

Golf Genie PRO is designed for PGA instructors on or off the course.

The app provides top tips for key shots and fixes for problem swings.

The app is all packaged up in an easy to use way, with 150 visuals for getting that shot just right.

# UTILITIES

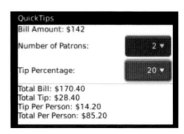

## CONVERSION COG

Conversion Cog converts a whole range of measurements.

In total, the tool features 627 units in 37 categories such as acceleration, area, blood sugar, clothes, cooking, currency and frequency.

The user interface is customisable too, so you can change the look of the app in just a few clicks.

## QUICKTIPS

Ever get stuck for how much to pay in a tip?

QuickTips allows you to easily work out how much tip you should pay, either when in a restaurant, in a cab or in almost any other scenario.

You can enter the tip percentage based upon which country you're in and a handy split bill allows you to split a bill between a number of people effortlessly.

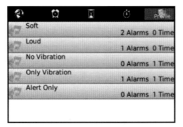

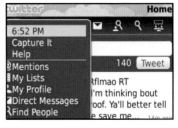

## WORLD CLOCK MULTI ALARMS

World Clock Multi Alarms allows you to set multiple alarms, a world clock, countdown timers and a stopwatch.

The app features an attractive and easy to use interface, making it the perfect option for your morning wake up call!

## MENUCLOCK

If you find it annoying when you can't find out the time from within an application, MenuClock is the perfect companion for you.

The app puts a clock into the menu of your BlackBerry, so when you press the BlackBerry key, you can see the time at the top of the menu.

Simple but effective.

## CALL CONTROL BLACKLIST LITE

Call Control Blacklist Lite allows you to block calls from people you really don't want to speak to.

It's not just manually entered phone numbers that can be blocked – you can also block calls from a community blacklist that includes spammers and FCC reported numbers.

## PC-KEYPAD

PC-Keypad allows you to control your BlackBerry from a PC.

It comprises an app for the BlackBerry and a PC side application.

Connect your BlackBerry via USB and perform all your usual functions with the benefit of a larger keyboard.

## CALL LATER AUTOSEND SMS

It can be annoying when you receive a call but are too busy to answer.

Call Later AutoSend SMS allows you to send an SMS to the caller to say you're busy but will return the call in a specified time. Just press the ignore button and select a predefined message to relay to the caller.

## SMARTGUARD PRO

SmartGuard PRO features real-time anti-virus, an anti-SPAM filter, Call blocker, Anti theft and recovery with GPS tracking, remote wipe, personal guardian and wireless backup and restore of data for your BlackBerry.

It's an all-in-one solution to keep your BlackBerry safe wherever you are!

# TRAVEL

## KAYAK

You may already know Kayak as an excellent Website for comparing flight, hotel and car rental prices and the Kayak app is a fast way of looking those up on the go; we like the way you can sort hotels by how cheap, close, classy or 'choice' they are (cute terms for ratings and amenities) and you can save search results on the site and see them on your phone.

## UBINAV

The slightly quirky interface shouldn't hide the fact that this is a capable satnav app; not only can you look up businesses anywhere in the UK and Ireland and get turn-by-turn navigation to points of interest and addresses (including from your address book) or two points you choose on the map, with 2D or 3D views of the route as you go – but you can also link UbiNav to Facebook and have it update your status when you leave, arrive or – more usefully – get stuck in traffic.

## NAVITA TRANSLATOR

Translate words and phrases using your choice of Google Translator, Google Dictionary or Bing Translator choosing between over 50 languages and copy the translations (or send them as a message or tweet). You can't say what you want translated but the app can read out translations in major languages in quite a reasonable accent.

## YELP

Where's the nearest chemist – and is it still open? Yelp isn't just for finding places to eat (although it's a reliable way to do that, with reviews from real people and a filer for only showing what restaurants are open right now); you can look up nearby banks when you need to get some cash out of the ATM, or find a church, a vet or a cobbler who can put the heel back on your shoe.

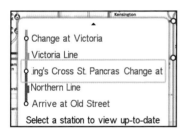

## XE CURRENCY

It's hard to keep currency rates in your head when you're travelling (or when you're shopping online).

You can tell at a glance with XE Currency. Scroll to the currency you want to convert from (the common ones are preset but you can add more) and type in the amount to see conversions for all the currencies listed at the latest rate. You can even type in a sum like 12.99*1.095 to get the amount including California sales tax.

## TUBE BUDDY

If you take the London Underground or Dockland Light Railway regularly, you need Tube Buddy to help you keep an eye on whether your journey home is going to be problematic. The simple interface shows you the status of all the lines (in alphabetical order, although you can reorder them) and you can also see live departure boards for individual stations.

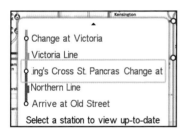

## TUBE MAP

If you need to use the London Underground and you don't know your way around London already, get Tube Map for browsing the map, planning your route (with an estimate of how long it will take and details of how well each line on your route is running) or just finding the nearest tube station by GPS.

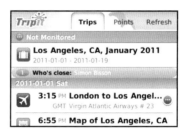

## TRIPIT

If you use the free TripIt service to track your travel reservations (forward the booking confirmation emails for hotels, flights and rental cars or fill in trip details by hand), you can see the details where you need them. Look up airport terminal maps, get tips on the best seat, click through to check in online – and see if anyone you know on TripIt is travelling to the same place.

# WEATHER

## WEATHERBUG

WeatherBug may not have the slickest interface but you get an excellent range of information with details of current conditions and a seven-day forecast (with an overview or details).

You can search for locations you want regular reports from or scroll across the map and press and hold to get an instant weather report for any location.

## THE WEATHER CHANNEL

A really comprehensive weather app although without the beautiful graphics of BeWeather; hourly, 36-hour and ten day forecasts, maps details of weather at local airports and severe weather alerts.

You can add a link to the calendar and contacts but (disappointingly) it only looks up locations you've already chosen.

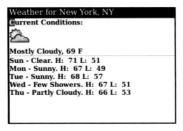

## INSTANT WEATHER

Instant Weather is actually a convenience key launcher disguised as a weather app.

You can assign any weather app to the convenience key but, especially on the Torch where you have only one, you may want to use that for another app.

Click the convenience key twice to see the weather and assign two favourite apps, phone numbers or tasks.

## WEATHER EYE

This is a comprehensive weather app from the Weather Network that gives you detailed forecasts.

The current weather information includes a 'feels like' temperature that takes things like humuidity and wind into account, plus there's an hourly forecast, a detailed short term forecast, overview forecasts for the next five days and a map view.

## BEWEATHER

Track ten cities plus your current location (by GPS).

There are full and compact views of the next 12 hours or 7 days plus views of the current weather that add details like sunrise, sunset and moon phase, humidity or daily or hourly.

Even the app icon shows your choice of temperature and conditions.

## WEATHERPLUS

If you'd rather have a basic weather forecast on your homescreen where you can see it quickly than detailed information buried in an app, WeatherPlus is ideal , especially on BlackBerry 6.

Choose where you want to see weather for and whether you want a five day forecast or just the current details.

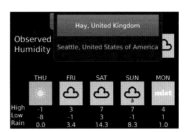

## NORTH FACE SNOW REPORT

North Face's Snow Report doesn't really count as an app; it's more of a widget that launches the Website – but the site is nicely tuned to work on the BlackBerry screen and has all the info you need to see if it's worth taking a last minute skiing break.

You can set your ten favourite resorts and see the snow fall and forecast, look at trail maps and get a map to the resort.

## WEATHER TRAX

About as basic as a weather app can be, Weather Trax just shows current conditions, temperature and humidity with a five day forecast that includes high and low temperatures and chance of rain.

What is useful is how easy it is to add multiple locations and switch between them from the on-screen menu – try it if you need something ultra-simple.

# CHAPTER SEVEN

**Multimedia**

EDGE

**12:21**PM
Thursday, May 22

(3) Messages

# CAMERA INTERFACE

**T**he latest iteration of the BlackBerry OS, BlackBerry 6, brought with it a range of enhanced, user-friendly multimedia features. This fine tuning includes tweaks to the way the camera operates that makes it even easier for users to get the photo results they want, when they want them.

A range of camera modes are also on offer. Take a look at the diagrams to find out more about how the new camera interface works on both touchscreen and non-touchscreen BlackBerry smartphones.

"With BlackBerry 6, we focused on perfecting the point and shoot experience. Users can capture photos quicker and better than ever before with a variety of new features in BlackBerry 6. New onscreen controls means there is no need to hunt through menus for your favorite options," product manager Vikram wrote on the official BlackBerry blog. "You will be able to access and review camera pictures, set popular options and pick from a variety of scene modes, all directly from the camera screen. You will also be able to capture video using the video camera application on the device."

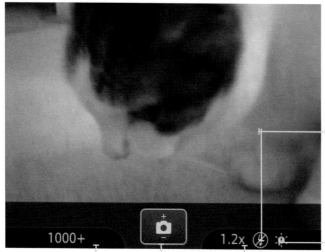

**FLASH STATUS**

**LOW LIGHT WARNING**

1000+   1.2x

**NUMBER OF PICTURES REMAINING**
This details how many photos you can still fit on your phone or memory card

**ZOOM/TAKE PHOTO**
Slide your finger up and down to zoom in or out and press the button to take the photo

**ZOOM LEVEL**

## ZOOM
Control zooming in and zooming out by tapping the + or -

## PICTURE GALLERY
This icon will take you to your picture gallery or previous pictures taken on the device

## SCENE MODES
Choose from a number of scene modes including auto, face detection, portrait and sports

## FLASH
Tap to turn the flash on or off

## GEOTAGGING
Add your location to your image by tapping this key

## SHUTTER BUTTON
Tap this to take the photo

# MUSIC ALBUM ART AND DISCOVERY

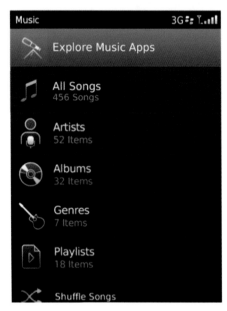

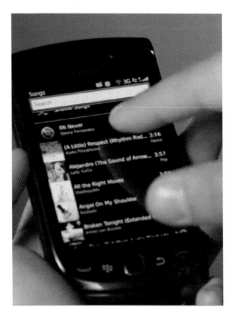

**B**lackBerry smartphones of late have proved themselves as more than just competent media players. Often, they've given standalone portable media and MP3 players a run for their money.

Their popularity is largely due to the familiar functions and interface on each device and the sheer usability that BlackBerrys both high and lower end boast.

With BlackBerry 6, it's all about the look and feel. Users are greeted with album art to make their listening and viewing experience even more intuitive and engaging.

In addition to the syncing capabilities of BlackBerry's latest desktop software, users can also quickly and easily look at their entire music catalogue (either iTunes or Windows Media Player-based) at a glance on their BlackBerry. This is thanks to a feature called Wi-Fi Music Sync, which lets them create and

edit playlists and select tunes to download.

"The minute you've loaded your music library to your BlackBerry smartphone via BlackBerry Media Sync, you'll notice that we've added album art virtually everywhere for instant and easy recognition of your favorite albums," the official BlackBerry blog states, as well as bigging up the ease of navigation provided by the interactive carousel. To select and browse through your music collection, you simply swipe this carousel and watch it move along.

It's also easy to sniff out tunes by the same artist or from the same album whenever or to find music/video/images if you don't already have a collection. To do so you just need to head to the media player's main menu and select **Explore Music Apps**, **Explore Video Apps** or **Explore Picture Apps** depending on what it is you want. You'll then be guided to links for the most popular apps in the App World relating to your search.

# PODCAST APP

Discovery Channel Video Podca...

A s we've implied elsewhere in this guide, BlackBerry is more than just a nice-looking device or solid business tool – it's a total platform comprising software, hardware, apps, services and more. There's a host of cool features on offer with the latest version of the BlackBerry OS and in this section we want to outline what the new podcast app can do for you.

The podcast app is pre-loaded with BlackBerry 6 and allows users to search, sign up to and enjoy podcasts (both audio and video) while out and about using their BlackBerry smartphone.

As well as ensuring you don't miss out on your favourite podcast simply because you're not near your desktop PC, this handy app also allows you to browse for and subscribe to new podcasts as and when your tastes and requirements change. Whether it's a film, arts update or the news, there's something available for everyone.

BlackBerry smartphones that ship with Blackberry 6 OS will come with the podcast app ready to rock and roll. But you can still benefit if not. After double checking you meet the system requirements below, simply enter your email address on the BlackBerry website and a download link will wing its way to you or visit the App World and download it from there.

## SYSTEM REQUIREMENTS
- A supported device: BlackBerry Bold, BlackBerry Curve, BlackBerry Pearl, BlackBerry Storm, or BlackBerry Tour.
- An active data plan that includes web browsing.
- A microSD card if required by the handset in question.

# ORGANISE YOUR PHOTOS

Once you've taken pictures using your shiny new – or trusy old, even – BlackBerry, you'll want to ensure you can find them when you need to quickly and easily – for your own use or to share with friends and family. After all, you've captured the memory so you don't want to lose it by having to sift through thousands of random file names do you?

It won't be a surprise to hear that BlackBerry has this covered. BlackBerry Media Sync does just what you'd expect with a name like that. And more, of course. It's not just about syncing and uploading images and such like as we've already outlined elsewhere in this guide.

In addition to importing images, you have complete control over how little, or how much, of your snap portfolio is transferred over from your BlackBerry to your desktop and vice versa.

The good news doesn't end there. The latest version of the BlackBerry OS and associated desktop software also makes the photographic experience – from shooting your subject to editing and then storing – even better.

"With BlackBerry 6, we will also provide multiple dynamic ways to view and organise your photos, so thousands of photos can be organised intuitively. For example, photos will be able to be grouped by event or by date. You will be able to view the full picture or a slide show of pictures with transitions," the company claims.

"BlackBerry smartphones with touch support are designed to easily zoom in on an area of interest with the "Pinch to Zoom" feature. BlackBerry 6 will also allow you to select groups of pictures to share, copy, paste or delete."

It's also easy on the device itself, particularly when it comes to sharing your images with friends, family, colleagues or the rest of the world:

- On the home screen click **Media** > **Pictures**
- Using the icons, either create a new folder or look at your images in slide show view.
- To share your snaps, click on the envelope icon and then select whether you would like to send it via email or MMS.
- Then compose an email and follow the instructions if you need to adjust the image size.

To create new folders and move images to and from folders:

- On the home screen click Media > Pictures
- To create a new folder, select the Menu button then New Folder
- You will then be given the opportunity to name the folder. Click OK. Your new folder will then be created.
- To add items to a folder, click on an image, then select the Menu button and Move To Folder option. Select the folder you want to move the image to and then Move Here
- You can also use the cut, copy and paste options or by synching.

It's also very easy to assign images to contacts, set as wallpaper, view as a slide show or just look at the picture's properties all from within the menu. Of course, you can also quickly and easily search for images too. After you've named or renamed them, that is, which is also a doddle thanks to the intuitive menu.

# STREAMING, SHARING AND SEARCHING FOR VIDEOS

**M**odern BlackBerry smartphones are multimedia powerhouses, designed to help you get the most out of your mobile experience whether you're at work or play. In addition to solid email, productivity and management considerations that will ensure you can keep pace with office life while out and about, there's plenty on offer to help you wile away the commute to work or just relax and forget about corporate life altogether.

Video, much like the rest of the new imaging features on offer with BlackBerry 6, is quite something. In addition to being able to shoot, edit and share your own videos, you can also download and watch content on the move as well as streaming to your handset.

## MEDIA SYNC

As we've already outlined, the latest versions of BlackBerry Desktop Manager and Media Sync include features that make it easy for you to turn your BlackBerry smartphone into a video-watching tool that will rival many of today's portable media players (PMPs).

The two-way video sync included with Media Sync 6.0 makes synching between your BlackBerry and PC a breeze. This has dual benefits: It means you can take clips from your desktop computer wherever you go by transferring to your BlackBerry as well as backing up and storing video you've taken using your BlackBerry on your PC.

For more information on synching your

BlackBerry video content with your PC or Mac, don't forget to check out the relevant chapters in this guide.

## SEARCHING MADE EASY

Once you've spent time and effort perfecting your Spielberg-esque skills and shooting video using your BlackBerry, you'll want to be sure you can find it again easily. Whether that's to show off to your friends or just for ease of reference is up to you, but whatever the reason, you'll be pleased to hear the search process is a cinch.

"Searching through videos on your BlackBerry smartphone has been made easier in BlackBerry 6 with the new thumbnail view," according to the official BlackBerry blog.

"There will also be more ways to view videos in BlackBerry 6. You will be able to opt to play video in various sizes (Original, Fit to Screen, Full Screen), plus instantly share your videos with the world using the new integrated YouTube video uploader."

Who doesn't love YouTube? It's certainly one of those applications that can see you spending hours looking through video funnies without realising just how much time has passed. Now you can do the same on the move, whether you're waiting for a plane, on a train or just trying to keep occupied in between meetings (though if your boss asks, we didn't suggest that!).

By hitting the YouTube app icon, you'll be prompted to either upload a video to the site or to visit the mobile version of YouTube itself.

Let's not forget the Universal Search feature of

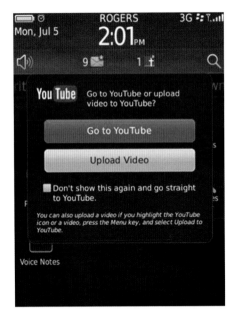

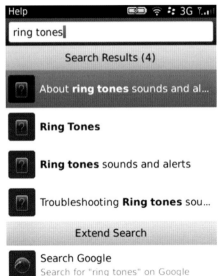

BlackBerry 6 OS. It lets you search for anything you like, quite literally. And that, naturally, includes video too. You can search for video content already stored on your handset, or you can try and find something completely new. Just hit the magnifying glass, type video or something more specific and Universal Search will do the rest for you.

You can also opt to use the Explore Video Apps option within the media player's main menu. This will guide you to the most popular video in BlackBerry App World so you can see what everyone else is raving about.

## IT'S GOOD TO SHARE

Those familiar with YouTube will already know you can share the videos you like the most with friends quickly and easily. But you can take sharing one step further by sending your own videos onto friends or uploading to social networking sites quickly and easily.

The BlackBerry Connections newsletter has some handy tips and hints to walk you through the sharing process. And once you've done it once, you'll be able to do it in your sleep. It really is that easy.

To share video already stored on the BlackBerry:
- Fire up the Media browser, enter Videos
- Select the video you wish to share
- Press Menu
- Choose whether you want to send the video by Bluetooth, email or MMS.

To share a video you've just shot:
- Capture your video as normal
- In the Pause Recording menu opt for the Send Video envelope icon
- Choose whether you want to send the video email or MMS.

## BLACKBERRY VIDEO STREAMING

We've already outlined just how easy it is to watch videos on the move on your BlackBerry thanks to the new YouTube app. But for those who want more of a range of video options, there are a number of other streaming apps that can help.

By heading to http://appworld.blackberry.com/webstore/ and selecting the Photo & Video category, you'll be able treated to a choice of video sharing, editing and streaming apps to enhance your BlackBerry video viewing experience.

One such app that could be of interest is QIkInc's Qik Live Video Streaming. This handy app transforms lets you share events with your friends, family and colleagues. It's certainly handy for sharing early baby memories with relatives, keeping your friends updated on your travels or briefing your far-away colleagues on that important business meeting. All at the click of a button. You'll need to ensure you have version 4.3.0 or higher of the BlackBerry OS and that you have 363KB of space for the app, but it's well worth downloading if you meet that criteria. Best of all, it's completely free!

# CHAPTER EIGHT

## Tips and Tricks

# HANDLING ATTACHMENTS

**T**here is no escaping just how much email has become part of our everyday lives. This mode of communication is used to aid us both at work and in our leisure time and email-equipped smartphones have become almost like a best friend, keeping us connected to the world of work and/or play at all times.

The content of emails are very important to us as recipients and senders alike, but email attachments are also pretty key.

Many viruses are transmitted through attachments. This can spell bad news for users if not handled properly. In the desktop world we are advised not to open any attachments that come from unknown sources, just in case they contain something that wants to make our machine feel icky. It's the same story when it comes to mobile devices.

With the BES, attachments are encrypted using the same type of security used for your corporate emails.

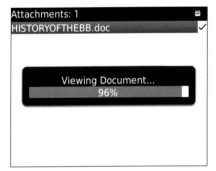

HISTORYOFTHEBB.doc (29K)

**Attachments: 1**
HISTORYOFTHEBB.doc ✓

Viewing Document...
96%

**HISTORYOFTHEBB.doc**

he story of the BlackBerry began more than a quarter of a century ago, when engineering students Mike Lazaridis (now co-chief executive) and Douglas Fregin founded Research In Motion (also known as RIM) in Canada, in 1984.
The company's early work focused on solutions and devices for the Mobitex wireless, packet-switched, data communications network in North America. Mobitex allowed for two-way, low-

There is a bit of a learning curve involved in teaching your BlackBerry how best to handle attachments. But it's a fast learner.

When you receive mail, you will have no problem viewing the email itself and the body copy, but you will also be told the name of any attached file, how big it is and what sort of file it is. That's as much as your BlackBerry will share with you until you tell it otherwise.

You must choose to download the attachment to see what you have been sent. But you don't have to open it. Indeed you can opt to open everything or view a table of contents to help you to make up your mind as to your next move.

Sometimes, it's necessary to make sure the BlackBerry attachment application is installed so the device is aware of what policies and procedures to follow when it comes face to face with an attachment. According to the official BlackBerry website, the following are all OK for your handset:
➔ Microsoft Office Excel, PowerPoint and Word.
➔ Corel WordPerfect.
➔ Adobe PDF.
➔ ASCII documents.
➔ HTML attachments.
➔ Images: JPG, BMP, GIF, PNG and TIFF.

You can open any of the above file types even if they have been compressed into the .zip format.

In much the same way a desktop machine's performance is affected by how much you've downloaded, downloading attachments can impact how your device functions. Thankfully expandable microSD storage means most BlackBerry smartphones will ensure you don't use up all of the memory on your handset, letting it perform at its best for a long time to come.

# PDF SUPPORT

**O**ut of the box, BlackBerry smartphones support basic PDF handling. But we live in a complex world where basic doesn't cut it all of the time. If you want more advanced formatting and image handling, there are a number of options available to you in the form of third-party applications.

What's more, the majority of them offer a trial period of the product before you have to stump up any cash, an added bonus that lets you try before you buy.

Please note: Some of these applications may not be compatible with all BlackBerrys. Please check before purchasing.

## DOCHAWK PLATINUM

As well as presenting PDF files in their original form, with embedded fonts and images intact, DocHawk is compatible with more than 55 different types of file formats.

It has several extra features, such as thumbnail previews and turbo scrolling, that make working with the files easier. The zoom feature, for example, reduces the number of clicks needed to move in and out of a document.

This all comes together to provide an app that enhances the user experience so that, aside from the smaller screen, you'd be hard pushed to even know you were viewing a PDF on a mobile device.

DocHawk integrates directly with the BlackBerry email pull-down menu, while PDF bookmarks and hyperlinks are also supported by the application.

There's even more to like about the app as, in addition to a three-day trial, you can choose how long you want to commit for. It's available – from www.terratial.com/products/dochawkplatinum - on a subscription basis, with three-month and one-year options available for $19.95 and $59.95 respectively. During the subscription period, you'll

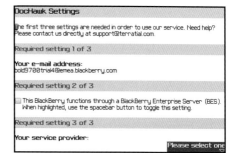

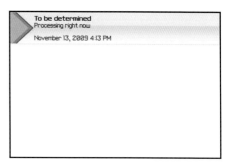

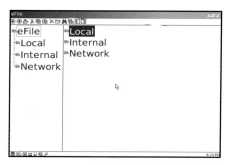

also receive any software updates and on-going technical support.

## EOFFICE

eOffice is based on four tenets: edit, view, access and share. It essentially gives users access to a mobile office while on the move, supporting Microsoft Word, Excel, PowerPoint, PDF, CSV, faxes and images, and files can be viewed exactly as they were designed to be seen on a desktop computer.

You can zoom in on PDF files and the document views are highly optimised for your handset, allowing you to browse through files without the annoying lag that often besets PDF file viewing on a mobile device.

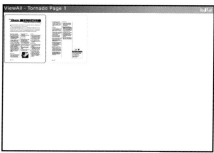

A new version of the software is now available, which its makers claim boasts an improved user interface that ensures easy access to the features that matter most.

What's more eOffice also offers users access to unlimited online document storage. All in all, we've found this app to be one of the cheaper options for adding advanced PDF support to your BlackBerry device.

## REPLIGO PROFESSIONAL

RepliGo Professional enables users to view email attachments such as PDFs, Microsoft Office, WordPerfect and OpenOffice files, faxes and photos. Innovative page re-flowing technology that makes document reading a speedier experience and akin to that of a desktop, means this app is a must have for those who spend a great deal of time working with such documents on the move.

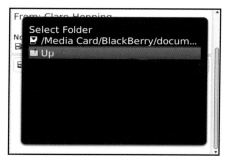

Users can zoom in to see details such as embedded fonts, graphics and tables, while support for hyperlinks and document tags within PDF documents gives you quick access to information.

The latest version – 2.1.0 – was released in August 2010 and boasts a number of new features such as support for devices running BlackBerry 6 OS, faster rendering of shaded objects and enhanced bookmark navigation among other things.

The app is available from www.cerience.com/products/pro/blackberry

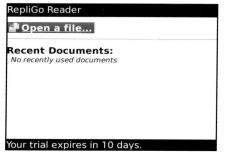

# EMAIL MANAGEMENT – BEST PRACTICE

**T**echnology is a double-edged sword. It brings us a number of benefits but they often come hand in hand with challenges. The BlackBerry is no exception. While it offers us 24/7 access to a world of communication, it's sometimes hard to switch off. Answering the hundredth email when you're meant to be enjoying a romantic meal with a loved one isn't really on. And a holiday should involve at least some downtime away from the hustle and bustle of work email.

According to research firm The Radicati Group, there were some 1.4 billion email users worldwide in 2009. This figure is expected to grow to around 1.9 billion by 2013. During the same period, the volume of messages sent on a daily basis will surpass 500 billion.

Given that The Radicati Group believes around 81% of current volumes is spam and that it costs a typical 1,000-seat business around $1.8million-plus a year to manage, email management and best practice is key.

It's not practical to just switch your phone off and hope the world goes away. The best way to ensure your own time stays your own time is to effectively manage your emails.

The most effective way of doing this is to turn off notifications unless you are waiting for an urgent message and check your BlackBerry only when you have free time. If you really can't help yourself, make use of the 'Auto On/Off' setting.

Having one inbox for all of your messages is very convenient. But it also means even more messages on screen at once, which can present somewhat of a management headache.

## FILING MESSAGES WITH BES

With BES you can clear out your inbox by filing messages into folders; simply click on the message and choose 'File'.

The most recent versions of BES will allow you to file the message in other mail tools, such as Outlook. But if you want to see the messages you file through Outlook as well, you'll need to synchronise that folder to your BlackBerry.

You can set up this using 'Redirector Settings' in the BlackBerry Desktop Manager by choosing **Advanced** > **Folder Redirection** > **Selected Folders** > **Choose Folders**. Alternatively, on your BlackBerry, choose **Options** > **Email Settings** > **Folder Redirection**: choose your mailbox, then your inbox and select 'Expand'. Now you can select individual folders to sync and choose 'Change Option' for each of them. Remember to open the menu and click 'Save' when you are done.

If you're a BIS user, you can only file messages into folders you create on that website – and filing messages there won't put them into folders in any other email tools (apart from the operator website). On the site, choose **'Manage Folders'** and click **'New'**. Give the folder a name and decide whether

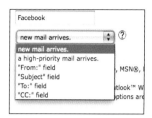

you want to automatically delete old messages; if you do, set the **'Auto-ageing'** options. You will now be able to file messages in a folder by clicking on them and then use **'View Folder'** to switch to the folder.

## FILTERING MESSAGES

You can use filters to prevent messages from appearing on your BlackBerry.

If you subscribe to a mailing list – or you don't want to see messages from, say, Facebook or a particular person – you can create a filter that sends the header, but not the message, or that stops the message altogether.

With BES, you can set up filters using the BlackBerry Desktop Manager, under **Redirector Settings** > **Filters** > **New**, or with your BlackBerry under **Message Options** > **Email Filters** > **New**. If you use the BlackBerry Internet Service, click the Filter icon (next to your email account on the website) and click 'Add Filter'.

Whichever way you do it, the options are the same. Give the filter a name and choose whether to filter by subject or by the 'from' address, then type keywords or the address to look for in the 'Contains' line. Choose 'Do Not Forward Messages To Device' and save the filter.

Instead of blocking certain messages from your BlackBerry and receiving everything else, you can decide which messages you want to see and block the rest. This means adding a filter for every new contact you want to hear from and it's a system that won't suit everyone. To make it work, you need to change the default filter for the account.

On the BIS site, select an email account and change the option 'When No Filters Apply' to 'Do Not Forward Messages To Device'. In BlackBerry Desktop Manager, look under **Redirector Settings** > **Filters** > **Forward Messages To BlackBerry Device** or, on your BlackBerry, look under **Message Options** > **Email Filters** for the default filter. Now you can set up filters for every address and subject line you want to read on your BlackBerry; simply choose 'Forward Message To The Device' as the action for each new filter.

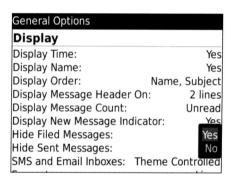

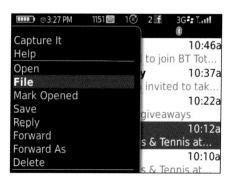

# TYPING SHORTCUTS AND CUSTOMISATIONS

**B**lackberry smartphones are productivity boosters, saving you tme and helping you to get more done while on the move. The platform also boasts a number of shortcuts to help you open apps, send messages more quickly and more.

## MESSAGING SHORTCUTS

These shortcuts can be used in a message:

| DESIRED ACTION | SHORTCUT |
|---|---|
| Reply to a message | Press R |
| Reply to all | Press L |
| Forward message | Press F |
| File highlighted email message | Press I |
| View email address of a contact in a message | Highlight the contact and press Q. To view the display name again, press Q |

These shortcuts can be used in a message list:

| DESIRED ACTION | SHORTCUT |
|---|---|
| Open a highlighted message | Press 'Enter' |
| Compose message from the message list | Press C |
| Mark a message as opened or unopened | Press 'Alt' and U |
| View received messages | Press 'Alt' and I |

| DESIRED ACTION | SHORTCUT |
|---|---|
| View sent messages | Press 'Alt' and O |
| View voicemail messages | Press 'Alt' and V |
| View Short Message Service (SMS) texts | Press 'Alt' and S |
| View call logs | Press 'Alt' and P |
| View all your messages again | press 'Escape/Back' key |

These shortcuts can be used to move around a message list:

| DESIRED ACTION | SHORTCUT |
|---|---|
| Move to top of screen | Press 'Shift key and 'Space' |
| Move to bottom of a screen | Press 'Space' |
| Move to top of a message list | Press T |
| Move to bottom of a message list | Press B |
| Move to next date | Press N |
| Move to previous date | Press P |
| Move to next unopened item | Press U |
| Move to next related message | Press J |
| Move to previous related message | Press K |

## BLACKBERRY USE MADE EASY

Built-in touches often missed by users, despite being in the manual:

| DESIRED ACTION | SHORTCUT |
| --- | --- |
| Insert a fullstop | Press 'Space' key twice |
| Insert @ and fullstops in email addresses | Press 'Space' key while typing in the address |
| Type an accent or special character | Hold the appropriate letter key and roll the trackball or track pad |
| Capitalise a letter | Hold the letter key until the capitalised version appears |
| Exit a screen or dialogue box | Press 'Escape/Back' button |
| Move the cursor in a different direction | Press 'Alt' key and roll the trackball or pad |
| Change an option field | Hold 'Alt' key. Click a value |
| Move to an item in a list or menu | Press the first letter of the item |
| Select a check box | Press 'Space' key. To clear the check box, press 'Space' key again |
| Select a line of text | Press 'Shift' and roll the trackball or optical pad |
| Turn on the backlighting | Press (don't hold) 'Power' button |
| Find contacts from the BlackBerry homescreen | Press the letter keys for the contact's first and last initials with a space between them |
| Switch to another program | Hold down BB button until programs appear. Toggle through to select |
| Move down a screen | Press the Space key |
| Move up a screen | Press Shift and Space |
| Multitask while on a call | Hold BB button, then homescreen. You can then access apps and emails |

## BLACKBERRY APPLICATIONS

These shortcuts can be used while in applications including Docs to Go and the BlackBerry browser:

| DESIRED ACTION | SHORTCUT |
| --- | --- |
| Change the size of a column in a spreadsheet | Press the W key |
| View the contents of a spreadsheet cell | Press 'Space' key with the cell highlighted |
| Search for text in a spreadsheet | Tap F followed by the text you're looking for |
| Switch to another worksheet | Press V and select another worksheet |
| Skip forwards through slides | Press N |
| Skip backwards through slides | Press P |
| Start a slideshow | Press S |
| Stop a slideshow | Press Escape |
| Enter new web address in browser | Press G |
| Add item to bookmarks | Press A |
| Show bookmarks | Press K |
| Refresh web page | Press R |
| Show list of last websites visited | Press I |
| Insert backslash to a web address | Press shift key followed by the space button |

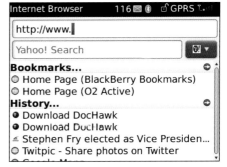

# HOW TO MAXIMISE BATTERY LIFE

**J**ust like other smartphones, the battery life of a BlackBerry can vary greatly, depending on how it's stored and how it's used.

That said, there are things you can do with your BlackBerry device to maximise the amount of time needed between charges.

In this section, we'll outline the hints and tips that will help you to get the most out of your battery and stop you having to carry around a charger or spare battery pack.

Before we share those secrets, the table on the right offers a quick rundown of the average battery life for a range of BlackBerry devices.

| BLACKBERRY DEVICE | AVERAGE TALK TIME (UP TO) | AVERAGE STANDBY TIME (UP TO) |
|---|---|---|
| **BlackBerry Torch 9800** | 5.5 hours | 17 days |
| **BlackBerry Bold 9700** **BlackBerry Bold 9000** **BlackBerry Bold 9780** | 6 hours 4.5 hours 6 hours | 17 days 13.5 days 17 days |
| **BlackBerry Storm 2** **BlackBerry Storm 9500** | 6 hours 5.5 hours | 11.5 days 15 days |
| **BlackBerry Pearl 3G 9105** **BlackBerry Pearl 8110** | 5.5 hours 4 hours | 18 days 15 days |
| **BlackBerry Curve** 8300, 8310, 8320, 8900 | 4 hours | 17 days |
| **BlackBerry Curve 8520** **BlackBerry Curve 3G 9300** | 4.5 hours 5.5 hours | 17 days 19 days |
| **BlackBerry 8800 series** | 5 hours | 22 days |
| **BlackBerry 8700 series** 8700g, 8700f, 8700v, 8707g, 8707v | 4-5 hours | 16 days |

Modern BlackBerry devices make use of Li-ion (Lithium-ion) batteries. These are rechargeable and rely on the movement of a lithium ion between the cathode and anode to provide power while in use and while charging.

One of the reasons Li-ion batteries are so popular is because they offer manufacturers a really good weight-to-energy ratio. They are also said not to adversely affect a device's memory or suffer from energy seepage when they are not being used – all important factors for today's demanding BlackBerry users.

Here are our top-six tips for ensuring the engine that powers your BlackBerry lasts:

1. Fully charge the battery before first use.
2. Don't wait until your battery is completely dead before recharging. Leaving it to the last minute may mean you don't have your BlackBerry in action when you need it most.
3. Turn off the Wi-Fi and/or Bluetooth/radio-searching capabilities of your BlackBerry if you don't need them. Otherwise, your device will constantly search for connectivity, tiring it out.
4. Keep an eye on the backlight brightness on your BlackBerry device. Reducing it a bit won't make much difference to the display, but it could make a noticeable difference to how long your battery lasts.
5. Store your BlackBerry at the right temperature. Heated environments will make your battery feel weaker much more quickly – like a tourist in a hot destination.
6. Social networking, email and gaming addicts beware! Intensive application use will drain your battery's juice levels quicker than anything else.

# CHAPTER NINE

# UNDOCUMENTED AND USEFUL FEATURES

**S**martphones generally live up to their names. They are often filled with handy tools, shortcuts and other time-saving features that mean business users and consumers alike have more time to do the things that matter to them most, whether work, rest or play.

The BlackBerry is no exception. In addition to the usual suspects of email, web browsing, connectivity options and multimedia support, you'll also find many built-in, time-saving shortcuts.

Designed to make using the BlackBerry as quick and simple as possible, these shortcuts will help you to type faster and ease navigation and file access. Some of them even remain undocumented by the manufacturer.

These are largely features left over from the testing process or are engineering functions that serve no useful purpose for everyday users. But that doesn't mean that they aren't of use full stop. In fact, they are certainly worth having a play with and we will tell you more about how your device works and whether it is running in optimum condition. The benefit of this definitely shouldn't be underestimated.

## SYSTEM INFORMATION AND HOW TO GET TO IT

The 'Status' feature in the Options menu provides basic information about the state of your device and its network connection. But there is much more information on offer, for example, logs that detail problems and operations that could help identify any issues you might be having or explain what your device is doing when you are not using it. This is known as the Event Log.

## TO ACCESS THE EVENT LOG

1. In the Applications screen hold down the **ALT** key and enter the sequence **LGLG**.
2. After a second or two, the Event Log will appear.
3. Within the Event Log, select an individual entry and click to view further details. You can also clear the log, which will free up a small amount of memory on your BlackBerry, or go into the Options menu to configure the types of event that are recorded in the log.
4. To close the Event Log and return to your home screen, choose 'Close' from the menu.

The next piece of 'hidden' information is not a secret feature, but it is one frequently overlooked by users. The 'Help Me' screen is a handy repository for key BlackBerry device data such as operating system version, battery level, wireless signal strength and available storage.

Event Log (Warning)

| W net.rim.scan - NeNa |
| W net.rim.scan - NNet |
| W net.rim.scan - NeNa |
| W net.rim.scan - NNet |
| a net.rim.gcmp - GCRp |
| a net.rim.gcmp - GCSp |
| W net.rim.scan - NeNa |
| W net.rim.scan - NNet |
| W net.rim.scan - NeNa |
| W net.rim.scan - NNet |
| W net.rim.scan - NeNa |

Event Information

| Name: | net.r |
| Severity: | V |
| GUID: | 60714307f9 |
| Time: | Nov 26, 2009 2 |

NNet

## TO ACCESS THE HELP ME SCREEN

1. Hold down the ALT+CAP+H keys in the Applications screen and the Help Me screen will appear.
2. Select 'Close' or press the back button to exit.

The standard signal-strength display on a BlackBerry uses five bars to represent how much mobile network signal is available at any particular time. However, it isn't very precise and your BlackBerry is capable of giving you far more detailed signal information. If nothing else, this information could eliminate/confirm a weak signal as the cause of odd device behaviour, such as a refusal to load web pages.

## TO ACCESS THE MORE DETAILED SIGNAL DISPLAY

1. On the home Applications screen, hold down the ALT key and enter NMLL.
2. The signal-strength display will change from the five-bar, graphical view to a more precise numerical value. This represents your signal strength in decibels (dB).
3. If you want to go back to the standard display, enter the same key sequence, ALT+NMLL.

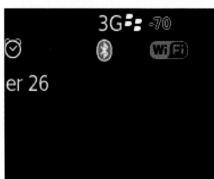

Smart System Codes also give users another great way of getting information about their device. Whenever you work in a default BlackBerry application, you can enter a Smart System Code into a text field. After entering the code and pressing 'Enter' or 'Space', the corresponding piece of information is displayed in a box on the screen.

| Smart code | Info returned |
|---|---|
| **myver** | Version of the device and its software |
| **LD** | Local time zone date |
| **LT** | Local time zone time *(useful when using an application that doesn't display the clock on the top bar)* |
| **mysig** | Shows data you entered in 'Owner Information' screen in Options menu |
| **mypin** | Your device PIN (*not your SIM-card PIN*) |

## WORKING WITH APPLICATIONS

There are numerous keyboard shortcuts available that will help improve navigation and automate certain multistage tasks.

In addition to the general purpose shortcuts listed elsewhere in this guide many BlackBerry keyboard shortcuts are specific to the built-in applications, such as the email client, the calendar, address book and web browser.

The BlackBerry home Application screen also supports several shortcut letters to enable you to jump to different pieces of software. To use these on newer devices, you will first need to disable the 'Dial from Home Screen' option under **Options > General Options > Phone.**

This feature is on by default, allowing you to press keys to dial numbers or bring up address-book contacts. Turning it off means you will have to go into the Phone application (press the green dial button once) before typing in a phone number or contact name. When this feature is off, you are free to use the following keyboard shortcuts:

### Word To Go - Untitled.doc

Sat, Nov 14, 2009
12:17:56 PM
9700/5.0.0.321
pin:2125DC06

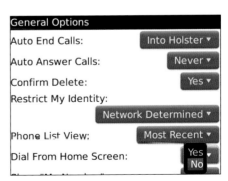

| Key | Application launched or feature activated |
|---|---|
| A | Address Book |
| R | Alarm Clock |
| B | Browser |
| U | Calculator |
| L | Calendar |
| C | Compose email |
| K | Keyboard lock |
| M | Messages |
| D | Notes |
| O | Options |
| P | Phone |
| F | Profiles |
| V | Saved Messages |
| S | Search |
| T | Tasks |
| W | WAP Bookmarks |

## CUSTOMISING THE ICON LIST

You can also customise the main home Application screen and any sub folders. And there's no need to keep the icons in the order in which they first appeared - great if you use one app more than the others.

The standby screen is the one your mobile reverts to after a period of inactivity, with six icons along the bottom, your wallpaper in the background and basic phone data (battery, signal, network information, time and date) along the top. You can have your most-used icons positioned here for easy access and, in the case of email, to see which mailboxes have new messages in them.

The icons on either screen can be rearranged, moved into folders or hidden. Here is one method that lets you move an application (in this case, the Contacts) from one part of the home Applications screen to another.

Moving Contacts

[1]  Highlight the Contacts application on the home screen and press the menu button.
[2]  Select 'Move' from the menu.
[3]  Move the icon around the home screen using the trackball or wheel. When you have found a suitable location, click the trackball to confirm.
[4]  The application is saved in the new icon location

The same process is used if you want to move icons into or out of folders; simply select 'Move to Folder' from the menu and choose the folder into which you wish to move the icon. To move an icon out of a folder, do the same thing, but select 'Applications' as the folder to move it to – this puts the icon back on the home Application screen.

The menu can also be used to hide icons you don't use, thereby reducing junk. Here, we will hide the Contacts application.

Contacts

[1]  Highlight the Contacts application on the home screen and press the menu button.
[2]  Select 'Hide' from the menu.
[3]  The application is now hidden from view – but it is still there.

To bring a hidden application icon back, press **ALT**+**trackwheel** and choose the Show All menu option. This restores all of the hidden icons.

## SWITCHING BETWEEN RUNNING APPLICATIONS

A BlackBerry can have multiple applications running at the same time and you can switch between them in a similar way to on a Windows PC or Mac. For example, if you are writing an email and need to query some information on the web or call someone, there are two ways you can swap between applications or return to the home Application screen to launch a new program.

Options

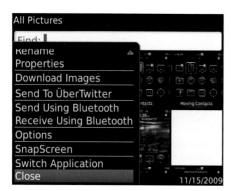

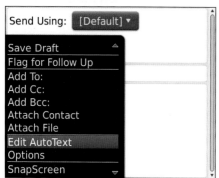

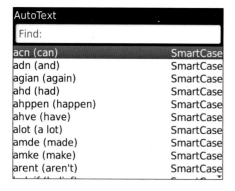

[1] Within most standard applications (the ones pre-installed on your BlackBerry) there is a menu option 'Switch Applications' (usually above the 'Close' option). Select this to bring up a ribbon display that shows currently running applications, along with the home Application Screen. Simply highlight the item you want and click on it.

[2] If the application you are running doesn't include the Switch Applications option – or it isn't convenient to access the menu display – there is a keyboard shortcut. Press and hold the **ALT** key and then press **ESC** (the back button). This will bring up the same ribbon of icons as the Switch Applications option.

## AUTOMATING YOUR TEXT

This is one of the easiest and most beneficial shortcuts, but, although it is a documented feature, it often gets forgotten by BlackBerry users. By using the AutoText feature, common typographical errors or shorthand can be automatically replaced with a full word or words. It is a huge timesaver and can be used to avoid having to type punctuation in commonly used words, as well as for correction purposes.

## TO ADD AN ENTRY TO AUTOTEXT

[1] When typing an email or typing in any other standard application, press the menu key and select 'Edit AutoText' to get a list of pre-defined AutoText mappings.

[2] Press the menu again and select 'New'.

[3] Fill in the word you want to replace – let's say the word 'eBay' has been typed as 'eBya'.

[4] Fill in the word you want to replace it with – in this case, eBay.

[5] Select 'Save' from the menu and hey presto!

# CHAPTER TEN

## Security

**BlackBerry**

EDGE

 )))    3 ✉*    **12:21**PM
Thursday, May 22

    WiFi

(3) Messages

# DATA ENCRYPTION: KEEPING YOUR INFORMATION SAFE

**W**ith rapidly developing smartphones, they're becoming more sophisticated and more open to security threats, just like computers.

Like on a PC, smartphone data can also be hacked and stolen, or simply lost along with your phone.

The security you have on your smartphone should be as effective as it is on your computer - after all, you don't want top secret documents to fall into the hands of a competitor.

If you work in a regulated environment, such as financial services, you'll be liable for a fine or worse if it does. If there is unencrypted, personally identifiable customer data on your phone, such as an address or credit card details, you are in breach of the Payment Card Initiative (PCI) standards.

There is no technology to make people less likely to lose their phone, so encryption is the only way to protect data held on it. Even if the user doesn't immediately report their BlackBerry lost or stolen, anyone who finds the device can't read what is on it, giving the owner time to execute a remote wipe.

Data traffic between the BlackBerry Enterprise Server (BES) or BlackBerry Enterprise Server Express (BESX) and handsets is automatically encrypted.

By default, the server generates the master encryption key and the message key used to encrypt and decrypt the traffic.

Company IT administrators can also force their BlackBerry handsets to encrypt user and application data stored on the devices. Turning on content protection in the Content Protection Strength IT

policy rule in BlackBerry Manager, on the server, will protect calendar and contact entries, emails, memos and tasks, the browser cache and saved web pages, plus AutoText entries, in case these are used for legal 'boilerplate' or company details. For further security, set the Force Content Protection of Master Keys IT policy rule, which will make the handset encrypt the master key it uses to encrypt those files.

Many BlackBerry handsets have memory-card slots, so don't forget to protect files on removable cards. Set the External File System Encryption Level policy rule and choose whether to use a randomly generated key, the device password or both to encrypt the files. You may also want to use the Disable USB Mass Storage IT policy rule to stop users putting their handsets into Mass Storage Mode. This mode allows files to be dragged directly on to the storage card using Windows Explorer, rather than transferring them through the BlackBerry Desktop Manager, but the files won't be encrypted.

Users can encrypt their own devices by choosing **Options > Security Options > General Settings > Content Protection** – this will protect files stored in their handset's internal memory. To encrypt files on the memory card, select **Options > Media Card** or **Options > Memory > Media Card Support**, depending on which version of BlackBerry software you have. With older versions, files will be encrypted if they are in the videos, music, pictures, ringtones and voicenotes folders. With version 4.7 or later, all audio, video and image files will be encrypted unless they are already protected by Open Mobile Alliance (OMA) DRM (.DCF, .ODF, .04A and .04V) standards.

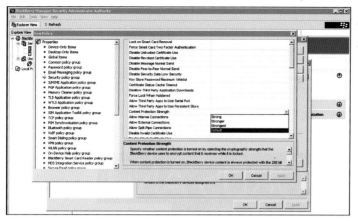

Force encryption of local files in the BlackBerry Manager by setting the Content Protection Strength IT policy rule.

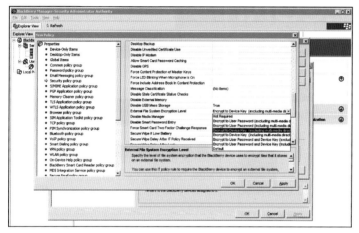

Use the External File System Encryption Level IT policy rule to make sure files on memory cards are protected.

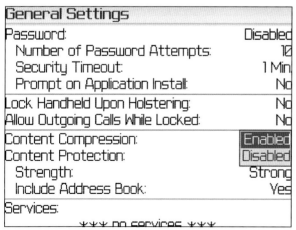

Turn on encryption of files on your own BlackBerry by setting the Security Options.

# PASSWORDS AND PIN SECURITY

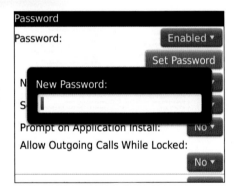

| Password | |
|---|---|
| Password: | Enabled / Disabled ▾ |
| | Set Password |
| Number of Password Attempts: | 10 ▾ |
| Security Timeout: | 30 Min. ▾ |
| Prompt on Application Install: | No ▾ |
| Lock Handheld Upon Holstering: | No ▾ |

| Password | |
|---|---|
| Password: | Enabled ▾ |
| | Set Password |
| New Password: | |
| | |
| Prompt on Application Install: | No ▾ |
| Allow Outgoing Calls While Locked: | No ▾ |

**A**lthough information sent to your BlackBerry is encrypted to prevent other people from accessing it, when it gets to your handset, encryption won't keep the data safe unless you lock your device with a password.

Depending on which version of the BlackBerry software you have, you can set a password by choosing **Options** > **Password** or **Options** > **Security Options** > **General Settings**. Change the password setting to 'Enabled', then press the menu key and choose 'Save'. The BlackBerry will ask you to type in a password and confirm it; after this, you will have to type in this password every time you turn on your handset.

Your BlackBerry password has to be between four and 14 characters long, and you can't have a sequence such as 12345 or repeat the same letter several times – the device will reject it because it's too easy to guess. Use a mix of letters and digits, but don't use obvious words or numbers (such as your name, favourite pet or date of birth) – ideally, don't use a word that's in the dictionary. However, don't make the password so complicated you have to write it down. Taking the first letters of a sentence and combining them with random numbers will give you a secure password that's hard to guess, but that you can remember.

By setting the Security Timeout, you can choose how long your BlackBerry must be idle before it locks and you have to use your password again to start it. Don't make this such a short time that you are tempted to turn off the password, but don't make it so long that someone could pick up the handset after you have put it down and not need the password. The default time is two minutes and the minimum time is one minute – but if that's longer than the time you set for the Backlight Timeout, the password timeout won't kick in until after both. So, if the Backlight Timeout is two minutes and the Security Timeout three minutes, your BlackBerry won't lock for five minutes.

If you use the BlackBerry Enterprise Server (BES), you can push a policy to all of the handsets to enforce the use of a password and set their minimum length, force the BlackBerry to reject passwords with an obvious pattern of numbers or letters, choose how long users can keep a password without changing it, and set the minimum timeout and prevent users from changing that.

RIM has slightly tweaked the lock function on BlackBerry handsets in recent firmware iterations, including later versions of OS 5 and in OS 6. The lock button on the top of the handset will only lock the keys so you don't accidentally press them when you're not using your BlackBerry. You will not have to enter a password to unlock the device unless your security time out duration has passed.

To get round this, there are a number of options including:

1. Set the Password Timeout to something relatively short in Options > Security > Password > Lock After: 2 Min
2. Use the Password Lock icon on the homescreen.
2. Set the Password Lock to a convenience key. This way, you can ensure your BlackBerry is always protected from anyone browsing your device and finding sensitive data.

If you get your password wrong 10 times in a row, your BlackBerry will assume you are a thief and wipe itself. If you are concerned someone could guess your password within 10 tries, you should probably think up a more secure one, but you can also reduce the number of password attempts allowed under **Options** > **Password** or **Options** > **Security Options**>

**General Settings.**

Each BlackBerry has a unique eight-digit PIN that identifies the handset. This is different to the PIN code you use to lock the SIM. To set or change the SIM PIN – which stays the same if you put the SIM in another handset and means no-one can make calls with the SIM if you lose your BlackBerry – choose **Options** > **Advanced Options** > **SIM card**, then press the menu key and choose 'Enable Security'.

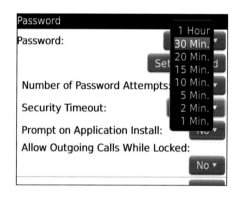

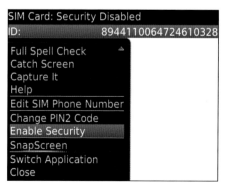

# SECURE NETWORK ACCESS

The connection between a BlackBerry handset and the BlackBerry Enterprise Server (BES) is secure and gives you Virtual Private Network (VPN) access to your internal network through the MDS Connection Service for most important applications. If you want to access files from a network, you will need a VPN client or a remote-access client.

However, MDS can also provide access to the internet, but is not optimised for use with the BlackBerry Browser included with BlackBerry 6, so may not work as it did on previous editions of the firmware.

Some Wi-Fi BlackBerry models, including the Curve, Bold, Storm and Torch, come with an Internet Protocol Security (IPsec) VPN client, but it's only for use over Wi-Fi connections. WICKSoft's Mobile Documents (previously known as Pocket VPN) is one of the few stand-alone VPN clients for the BlackBerry and can also access SharePoint and Exchange public folders.

Several remote-access clients for the BlackBerry use Windows Remote Desktop Protocol (RDP) for accessing specific PCs and servers through Terminal Services or Remote Desktop. There are Virtual Network Computing (VNC) clients as well, but RDP is a more efficient way of accessing Windows machines and doesn't need extra software on the PC or server. However, desktop PCs have to be left on for access and working on a smaller BlackBerry screen with applications designed for a full-sized PC can be challenging. Try TSMobiles (for server access) or RDM+ (for desktop access), available from *www.rdmplus.com*.

Rove's Mobile SSH tool allows terminals to emulate each other, so you can log into almost any server to administer it. If you are working with

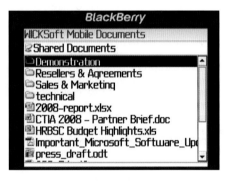

Windows servers, Rove's Mobile Admin lets you shut down and restart servers, view event logs, see printers and print jobs, unlock user accounts, view and edit shared files and folders, and manage drives, folders and files through a graphical interface that is designed to fit the BlackBerry screen rather than a PC monitor. It also includes RDP and VNC clients for emergency access.

Another alternative is to set up a remote-access proxy – such as PCXS's Condor File Explorer, Xenium eFile Server or Cortado Corporate Server – then run it on a server in your network and use Active Directory, with existing usernames and passwords, to control access, and the Mobile Data System in BES to encrypt the connection. The administrator can choose which folders and files are remotely accessible.

**Please note:** Not all of these solutions have been tested on all editions of the BlackBerry operating system and may not work as detailed here.

It is always best to check software is compatible with your particular BlackBerry model before purchasing.

# WI-FI SECURITY

**W**i-Fi is now available in most of RIM's devices, especially those at the higher end of the scale. When the Canadian manufacturer first began including wireless technology in its devices, people were concerned it would breach security. However, even if you use your handset with an unsecured Wi-Fi access point, the connection to the BlackBerry server is protected by 256-bit AES encryption. This applies to any business applications a company installs on a BlackBerry and to email, but it does not apply to web browsing.

To make Wi-Fi web browsing secure, you need to connect to an access point using encryption and all BlackBerry handsets with Wi-Fi support WPA (Wi-Fi Protected Access) and WPA2 personal and enterprise wireless encryption, which devices must have to get the Wi-Fi logo. This is much more secure than the original Wi-Fi security standard, WEP (Wireless Encryption Privacy), which was designed to offer the same minimal security available on a wired, Ethernet network once you are connected. Even with a 128-bit key, WEP can be cracked in a matter of minutes using freely available software.

Some insecurities have been found in WPA2 using the simpler Temporal Key Integrity Protocol (TKIP), but these don't let people eavesdrop on the network or connect without knowing the key, and they don't work at all on enterprise wireless networks using AES. To be completely secure, use a WPA2 key of around 20 characters, preferably random rather than common English words.

Wi-Fi-capable BlackBerry handsets also support WPS (Wi-Fi Protected Setup), a relatively new way of setting up secure wireless networks for the home by making it easier to configure the SSID of the network and to distribute the WPA2 encryption key. You type in a PIN rather than the whole key and, with version 4.6 of the BlackBerry software, the PIN is replaced by a push-button setup.

## Available Wi-Fi Networks

**SKY21844**
WPA-Personal

## Wi-Fi Security

Security Type:     Pre-Shared Key (PSK)

Pre-Shared Key: |

Back    Connect

Save

## Wi-Fi

Active Wi-Fi Connection:          None

☑ Prompt me when manual connection or login is required.

☐ Enable single profile scanning

## Saved Wi-Fi Profiles

* Empty *

# THIRD-PARTY SECURITY SOLUTIONS

**Y**ou don't need third-party software to securely use your BlackBerry, but if you need extra protection or specific security features, there's a range of tools to choose from.

RSA SecurID Authentication turns a BlackBerry into a SecurID token. Instead of paying extra for a hardware fob that generates a regularly changing number, which you then type in to authenticate your identity with a secure system, the SecurID software runs on the handset – although you still have to type in your username and token passcode. Arcot and Movilock also offer software that uses the BlackBerry as a multifactor authentication token.

BlackBerry email is secure and you can archive and log it through Exchange. But if you need to archive other types of message, GWAVA's Retail, Akonix's L7 Enterprise, Global Relay's Message Converter and Commondesk's Compliance Engine capture text, BlackBerry Messenger and PIN-to-PIN messages, webmail that goes through BIS and phone-call details.

Titus Labs' Message Classification tool labels messages, sent from a BlackBerry, that contain confidential or private information, while METAmessage ACT, from Onset Technology, can block messages, as well as archive any that get sent.

Email in transit is encrypted by BES and email on a BlackBerry can be encrypted by the device. But

if you want messages to be encrypted when they arrive on another email system, you need end-to-end encryption.

The PGP Support Package For BlackBerry automatically encrypts, digitally signs, decrypts and verifies PGP-secured emails. RIM's own S/MIME Support Package is an add-on to BES to support Entrust's Secure Messaging Solution; again, this lets you use the same Public Key Infrastructure (PKI) encryption on the BlackBerry as for desktop email clients.

Voltage SecureMail and Totemo TrustMail allow you to send encrypted messages to anyone, but they may need to view the messages through a web browser rather than in their email client.

You can use your BlackBerry handset as an encrypted USB drive with QuickVault's JumpVault software. As well as protecting files you manually copy, you can set up a schedule to copy specific folders and file types. There is also an option to remotely disable the software, but you pay extra for this service.

Alternatively, use the device's built-in encryption and BAK2u's PhoneBAK, or the GadgetTrak Mobile Security service, to send a remote SMS or email to your BlackBerry that will wipe your information and turn on an alarm. Both tools will also get the handset's location by GPS or cell-tower triangulation and text you if someone puts another SIM in it.

Administrators who want to control which files get copied on to devices, including BlackBerry handsets, need tools such as GFI's EndPointSecurity – although any endpoint security tool that controls USB devices should let you restrict file copying to a BlackBerry.

If you use Windows Rights Management (WRM) to control who can read, print or forward emails and Office documents, or for setting expiration dates, you will need a WRM gateway to let BlackBerry users access protected documents. GigaMedia's GigaTrust For BlackBerry lets them view protected information, while the Liquid Machines Gateway lets them send and receive protected messages and attachments.

If you use your BlackBerry for personal email and your mail service doesn't have particularly good spam filtering, check out Antair BlackBerry Spam Filter. This runs on your handset, so it works with any email account, and you can install a free trial directly on to your device from *www.antair.com/ota*.

**Please note:** Not all solutions have been tested on all editions of the BlackBerry platform.

Please check any software is suited to your particular BlackBerry device before purchasing.

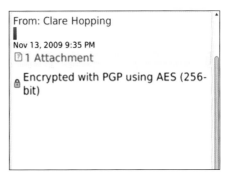

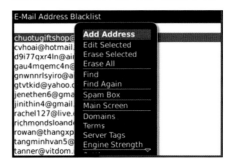

# CHAPTER ELEVEN

## Accessories

**vodafone UK**

**4:20**PM

Friday, December 19

SMS And M...   Contacts   Calendar   Browser

Vodafone...   Vodafone I...   Media   Clock

# CASES

### BLACKBERRY LEATHER HOLSTER FOR BLACKBERRY TORCH £24.99

Even if you take great care of your BlackBerry Torch 9800, it's more than likely you'll drop it or toss it into your bag, right next to your keys.

As with any device, the Torch can get scratched and to prevent that happening, RIM has designed the Torch 9800 Leather Holster to wear your device on your belt, so your phone is within reach at all times.

The case also includes technology that helps preserve battery power, while also recognising your in-holster notification settings and preferences.

### VAJA CUSTOMISABLE HANDCRAFTED CASES PRICE VARIES

If you want something a little more customised to hold your BlackBerry, Vaja offers a whole range that perfectly fit any battery.

The cases are all finished in leather and can carry whichever design you want.

Prices vary, but you can be sure you'll have a case to suit you and your taste, while perfectly fitting your BlackBerry, whether you keep it in a bag, pocket or on your belt.

### 9700 HARDSHELL CASE £19.99

The BlackBerry Hard Shell case snaps onto your BlackBerry Bold 9700 with a perfect fit, keeping it secure and the back safe from bumps and scratches.

Soft rubber side buttons make it easy to access the camera and convenience keys when in the case and there's easy access to all the main functions of your device including keyboard, headphone jack and volume keys.

# HANDSFREE

### BLACKBERRY WIRELESS
### HEADSET HS-500 £49.99

BlackBerry's wireless Headset HS-500 features a one-button design.

It allows you to easily answer, end, and mute calls, or activate voice dialing, whatever you're doing and wherever you are.

The volume automatically adjusts and background noise is reduced, so your calls and turn-by-turn directions can be heard loud and clear in noisy environments.

### PLANTRONICS VOYAGER PRO
### BLUETOOTH HEADSET £64.99

Plantronics' Voyager PRO is an advanced noise-cancelling Bluetooth headset, allowing you to clearly hear converstions.

Two noise-canceling mics are positioned on boom and there's AudioIQ2 technology with a 20-band equaliser, and three layers of WindSmart technology.

This makes sure you can be heard even in loud or intrusive conditions, whether you're in a bar or in gale force winds.

### VISOR MOUNT
### SPEAKERPHONE VM-605 £69.99

The BlackBerry Visor Mount Speakerphone VM-605 is an in-car solution that keeps your eyes on the road when on a call.

Because it fits on your car's sun visor, It's easy to use. Just clip it on, turn it on, and you're ready to start making and taking hands-free calls on the go.

The device also supports voice activated dialing, caller ID, and verbal notifications to let you know who's calling.

# SPEAKERS

## GEAR 4 BLACKBOX                    £69.95

The BlackBox from GEAR4 is a Bluetooth stereo speaker system. It features a hidden LED display and touch screen controls, so that nothing detracts from its elegance and minimalism, to make it look ultra sleek wherever you put it.

Simply link the speaker up to your BlackBerry and start streaming your music straight away.

## SUPERTOOTH DISCO PORTABLE BLUETOOTH STEREO SPEAKER        £79.95

The Supertooth Disco is a portable stereo speaker that allows you to listen to your favourite music wherever you go.

The SuperTooth Disco also includes a jack if you don't want to drain your battery and a subwoofer and speakers for a total sound power of 28 watts.

The Supertooth plays music up to 10 hours of non-stop music with one charge.

## LOGITECH PURE-FI MOBILE BLUETOOTH SPEAKERS & SPEAKERPHONE        £59.99

The Logitech Pure-Fi Mobile is much more than just a speaker. It also offers full call functions including making and answering phonecalls.

The speaker also comes bundled with a carrying case so you can take it wherever you go.

# EARPHONES

### ETYMOTIC HF2 £100
Etymotic is a master in sound and the HF2 is a perfect companion for your BlackBerry.

The headset works perfectly with the BlackBerry Curve, Bold and Pearl series, and with the custom fit earpieces, you can be sure they'll give you the best sound possible.

### SOUND ISOLATING 3.5MM HEADSET £24.99
We live in such a busy world that sometimes it's hard to focus. This sound-isolating headset lets you do just that, offering a superior sound experience in the process.

With noise isolating ear gels (available in three sizes), sound reproduction is accurate whether you're taking or making a call or listening to music or watching video.

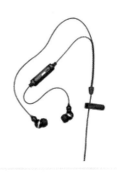

### MULTIMEDIA HEADSET £49.99
Offering highly optimised sound quality, thanks to cutting edge technology, design, comfort and manageability, this headset is ideal for those who want to block background noise out and audio in.

It boasts an elastomer cord with less tangle and multimedia controls, in addition to three interchangeable plates that let you customise your headset.

This is a premium multimedia headset. As such, you'd expect it to come with a premium price, but at less than £50 it's still not out of reach.

# OTHER ACCESSORIES

## BLACKBERRY MUSIC GATEWAY £44.99

The BlackBerry Music Gateway is not just another stereo product. It's, as the name suggests, the gateway to a whole other world of music as it lets you wirelessly stream the tunes on your BlackBerry through your home, car or portable sound system.

Using the Music Gateway is simple. Once paired with your chosen stereo system, the BlackBerry becomes a remote control and you become the DJ. And if someone calls you, the music automatically fades to alert you.

## BLACKBERRY 9700 CHARGING POD £10

The BlackBerry Charging Pod allows you to charge your BlackBerry while displaying your screen and giving you full access to your device.

When docked in the charging pod, your BlackBerry will display the time, and it looks pretty good too, whether postioned on your desk or on your bedside table.

## FIIO E5 HEADPHONE AMP £19.99

The Fiio E5 headphone amplifier is a perfect partner to your BlackBerry and earphones.

It's designed to improve the sound quality of your tunes and comes with a pair of mini-jack leads to plug the E5 directly into your phone or MP3 player.

Then, you just need to connect your normal earphone cable to the other end of the E5 There's a mini-USB socket, used to charge the amp's battery, a volume rocker, power button and the all-important bass boost switch.

# CHAPTER TWELVE

**THE FUTURE**

# THE FUTURE FOR BLACKBERRY

**B**lackBerry's parent Research in Motion (RIM) has been going strong for decades, serving up innovation after innovation after innovation.

It has a rich heritage of creating handsets and solutions that add value to users, both businesses and consumers alike. RIM recently - in 2009 - celebrated 25 years of innovation and 10 years of the BlackBerry and its solid history of innovation shows no signs of abating anytime soon.

To date approximately 115 million BlackBerry smartphones have been shipped, with the current subscriber base reckoned to be more than 50 million. What's more, the devices are in use across 150 countries, spanning some 400-plus networks, according to RIM. That's without even factoring in the impact that the respective arrival of the Torch and PlayBook will have on the market.

The company's results for its second fiscal quarter of 2011 (released in September 2010) were very buoyant, highlighting the platform's popularity. Revenue was up by 9% compared to the previous quarter and a whopping 31% higher than the same quarter the year before.

"RIM set another new record in the quarter by shipping over 12 million BlackBerry smartphones. This accomplishment and RIM's solid financial results during the second quarter were driven by effective business execution and strong demand for RIM's portfolio of BlackBerry smartphones and services in markets around the world," said Jim Balsillie, RIM's co-chief executive. "We expect a continuation of this momentum in the third quarter as we extend the rollout of new products including the BlackBerry Torch into additional markets and benefit from heavy promotional activities and increasing customer demand as we head into the holiday buying season."

Historically, BlackBerry was viewed as a tool for business users first and consumers second, but recent device launches have changed this mindset. This is backed up by RIM's 2009 annual report, which shows that some 60 per cent of subscribers added during the year were non-enterprise customers. That's not to say RIM has left the corporate world behind. In fact, far from it. In 2009,

the number of businesses using BES stood in excess of 175,000. This is a figure only set to grow.

RIM demonstrated significant innovation in the late 1990s and, while early handsets don't look much, they paved the way for RIM's future inventions, setting the pace and shape of the rest of the mobile marketplace along the way.

The company has always invested heavily in research and development to ensure the BlackBerry evolves and remains relevant, so what does the future hold for our favourite handset?

## GIVING USERS WHAT THEY WANT

It's clear RIM is listening to what users want. In addition to an array of form factors, input methods (hard keyboards, touchscreens and slimmed down key-sharing input), camera and connectivity options, handsets are also available both on contract and in prepay format.

2010 saw the launch of the stunning Torch, Bold 9780 and Curve 3G devices and the unveiling of a completely new form factor. The PlayBook tablet has created much excitement in both the consumer and business worlds and is likely to receive an even warmer welcome when it hits the market in 2011.

It would be pretty safe to assume that users will be treated to plenty more innovation, in the form of apps, devices and solutions in 2011 and beyond. When you consider that the device's humble beginnings were as a two-way, monochrome pager, it's come a long way.

Going forward mobile devices will become an extension of our personalities, whether at work, play or both. The mobile industry needs to move in this direction to satisfy our needs and consumers. RIM is no exception and will likely take on the other big mobile players when it comes to personalisation and customisation features on its handsets, both in terms of hardware and software.

## APP WORLD

BlackBerry's App World is one example of how RIM is trying to make the devices more useful to users. In addition to many pre-bundled applications, users can now download from a wealth of free and paid-for apps spanning a range of categories from business and travel to sport, weather and everything in between. Whoever you are and whatever your tastes, there's likely something to suit you here.

"The BlackBerry platform provides a truly unparalleled mobile experience for millions of people and we are thrilled today to enhance that experience with a new app store that helps connect consumers with developers and carriers," said Mike Lazaridis, RIM's president and co-chief executive, in a statement at the launch. "BlackBerry App World aggregates a wide variety of personal and business apps in a way that makes it very easy for consumers to discover and download the apps that suit them while preserving the appropriate IT architecture and controls required by our enterprise customers."

## A NEW OS
The arrival of BlackBerry 6 OS was a game changer. It brought with it new features, functionalities and opportunities for users and developers alike. However, it didn't just move the new in and the old out. Importantly, it kept all the good bits that users like and love about the platform and served up new bells and whistles on top.

The new goodies on offer with the OS include a redesigned interface, beefed up messaging functionality, enhanced browsing and a new, time-saving Universal Search tool.

"BlackBerry 6 is the outcome of RIM's ongoing passion to deliver a powerful, simplified and optimised user experience for both touch screen and keyboard fans," said Mike Lazaridis, RIM's president and co-chief executive. "Following extensive research and development to address consumer needs and wants, we are delivering a communications, browsing and multimedia experience that we think users will love, and we are thrilled to debut BlackBerry 6 on the amazing new BlackBerry Torch smartphone."

## TABLET-SHAPED FUTURE
The future for smartphones looks promising, but, with so much competition, RIM – and other mobile phone manufacturers – must continue to innovate to entice new customers and garner loyalty from their existing user base.

And innovative it has. The unveiling of the PlayBook was a surprise to some but a much-needed boost to others. Whilst built on a new tablet-focused OS, it will allow users to take advantage of a new platform with all the familiarity of BlackBerry they have come to know and love.

The news likely also proved a delight for developers too as it gives them another outlet through which to unleash their creativity and monetise the opportunity in the process.

While RIM is remaining tight-lipped on the subject, it wouldn't be ridiculous to assume that we may hear the pitter patter of tiny PlayBook feet in the future.

## EVOLUTION
RIM has made a lot of improvements to the handset in recent years, including colour screens with bigger displays, more memory and better battery life. BlackBerry users have also been treated to an array of form factors and inclusions, from 3G to Wi-Fi, GPS, Bluetooth and, now, tablet-style.

The BlackBerry is a very secure device, but increased security is still top of individual users' and companies' wish lists – and this issue will become increasingly important as mobile security threats continue to evolve.

We are putting more and more sensitive information on our mobile devices, which, in turn, are becoming increasingly key to our identities as individuals and representatives of our businesses.

As users, we need to be mindful of what data we store and how we store it, but we also look to handset manufacturers to do their bit. So RIM and other mobile manufacturers have to pre-empt and respond to the threats of tomorrow, today. Such security concerns have been addressed with the PlayBook and this is likely just the beginning of an even more secure journey for RIM and its fan base.

Looking towards the future, things are likely to continue to be shaped heavily by how users want to consume data and applications and take advantage of their devices as ways of enhancing their lives – whether at work or play. Users will get what they want and more so watch this space.

# GLOSSARY

## HSDPA
High-Speed Downlink Packet Access: an 'always on' improvement on standard 3G/UMTS data services. Offers download rates of up to 14.4Mbps, though most networks in the UK and the US offer 1.8, 3.6 or 7.2Mbps.

## CRM
Customer relationship management: Software to aid businesses in tracking and organising contact with current and prospective customers.

## ERP
Enterprise Resource Planning: A network-based solution that manages and coordinates a company's resources, information, and functions.

## SFA
Sales Force Automation: Software that allows a company to automate sales force management. Sometimes part of a CRM system.

## BI
Business Intelligence: Allows users to keep constantly up to date with company sales, product and organisational data while away from the office.

## GSM
Global System for Mobile communications: the most widely used digital mobile-phone system and Europe's de facto wireless telephone standard.

## GPRS
General Packet Radio Service: an 'always on' data connection for GSM mobile-phone services.

## EDGE
Enhanced Data for GSM Evolution: can provide near-3G data rates on a GSM network. Speeds of up to 384Kbps are possible.

## 3G (UMTS)
Universal Mobile Telecommunications System: the European version of the 3G wireless phone system. Offers data rates of up to 384Kbps.

## Wi-Fi
Generic term commonly used for wireless LAN technology, also known as 802.11a, b, g and n. Wi-Fi is a trademark of the Wi-Fi Alliance, which ensures the Wi-Fi compatibility of hardware.

## VoIP
Voice over Internet Protocol: the process by which voice telephone calls are made and carried across a data network rather than a conventional telephony system. Popular VoIP services include Skype, Vonage and Google Talk. Long-distance and international calls are usually much cheaper using VoIP than a conventional phone system.

## BES
BlackBerry Enterprise Server: a software plug-in for the most popular business email servers (Microsoft Exchange, Lotus Domino) that syncs email, calendar and address-book information between the server and any BlackBerry devices authorised to communicate with it.

## BESX
An alternative version of BES aimed at businesses who want the same capabilities but without the licensing and other overheads. It's a simple download that lets you enjoy the benefits straight away. It offers email management, security and more and, best of all, it's free!

## BIS
BlackBerry Internet Service: allows BlackBerry users to access the internet and POP3/IMAP email accounts without connecting through a BES.
The service is usually provided by mobile-phone operators.

### PLAYBOOK
RIM's first foray into the tablet computer space. The arrival of the PlayBook will bring RIM head to head with devices like the Apple iPad. RIM is remaining tight-lipped on its future tablet strategy for now.

### APP WORLD
The gateway to thousands of applications in a variety of categories to help users whether they're at work, at play or even on the beach. Apps are graded based on user opinion to help you make your mind up. Free and paid-for apps are available.

### POP
Post Office Protocol, also known as POP3: the most common and most basic form of consumer email account. Messages are downloaded from a server onto the client from a single mailbox.

### IMAP
Internet Message Access Protocol, also known as IMAP4: an improved standard for email used by consumers and businesses. Allows for multiple server-side folders and virtual mailboxes. Mail is retained on the server and synced with the client, so you always have access to the same set of emails. IMAP is the system behind most popular webmail services.

### Java
Industry standard, object-oriented language and virtual machine, invented by Sun Microsystems. Popular as a platform for mobile-phone applications because it can run as a virtual machine, making applications hardware-independent and able to run on multiple devices from different manufacturers.

### PDA
Personal Digital Assistant: a handheld computer, also known as a palmtop computer, which was

considered to be the forerunner of smartphones as we know them today.

### OS
Operating system: the core software, also referred to as firmware, that allows a mobile phone to function.

### PIM
Personal Information Manager: a software application that functions as a personal organiser.

### SIM
Subscriber Identity Module: a SIM card is the smartcard in all GSM and 3G phones. It identifies the user account to the network and provides data storage for basic user and network information, such as contacts.

### Bandwidth
The data capacity of a connection. A higher bandwidth can transmit more data over a given period of time.

### Bluetooth
A wireless standard that enables data connections between electronic devices such as desktop computers, phones, hands-free headsets and remote controls, usually within a 10m range, although some devices support over 100m.

### GPS
Global Positioning System: a receiver that communicates with satellites orbiting the earth to determine the position of people and objects on the ground.

### A2DP
A Bluetooth (see above) protocol that allows mobile users to stream music or video, wirelessly.